Testimonials

"I dwell in a make-believe world of shadows that I pretend to bring to life. Narayani, on the other hand, swims in oceans of love and is washed ashore time after time in cycles of rebirth that brings her a fulfilment that only very few special atmans have the good fortune to live and experience. In this marvelous little book she has written, Narayani entices you to swim with her and share in her joys and happiness, but at the end we are left lost at sea, in awe of a girl who dropped in to inhabit our shores and brought comfort and peace to those who needed her most. *My Heart Remembers* is an endearing, unashamed, and humble testimony to love and worship of a "King."

–Victor Banerjee, actor who portrays Paramhansa Yogananda in Swami Kriyananda's film The Answer

"This book is a beautiful gift of love to Swami Kriyananda and to all of its readers. Through the clear window of an open heart, it offers a personal glimpse of the last years of Swamiji's life."

–Nayaswami Devi, Spiritual Codirector, Ananda Worldwide, author

"I knew Swami Kriyananda for more than 40 years. In the last years of his life, I could not tune in to his consciousness without also feeling the spirit of Narayani, so completely had she surrounded Swamiji with her aura of loving care. Her spirit blended perfectly with his. This book is a spiritual classic. As the title says, right from the heart."

–Asha Nayaswami, author and renowned speaker

"This precious book made me alternate between laughter and tears. I think nobody can convey the heart and soul of Swami Kriyananda as Narayani can. He comes alive in these pages, just as he was: a humble saint, a noble king, a divine friend to all."

–Jayadev Jaerschky, author and spiritual teacher

"Narayani's book is a joy to read! Open and accessible, it provides valuable insight into Swami Kriyananda's last years on this earth. I hope it will help many people to tune in to Swami Kriyananda's living presence that can still be felt so immediately through his books, his music, and in the smiles of all his spiritual children."

–*Nayaswami Nirmala*, Spiritual Codirector, Ananda Sacramento

"Brought tears to my eyes many times. This is a story both personal and universal—a rare glimpse into the life and dedication of a saint. Deeply moving." –*Nayaswami Dharmadas*, Spiritual Codirector, Ananda Sacramento

"This book carries an energy which is sacred, strong, deep, from another sphere. Swami Kriyananda's energy and consciousness pass and work through this book with a transforming power. An active darshan!"

–*Cecilia Sharma*, founder, Ananda India Healing Sangha

"Seeing Swami Kriyananda through Narayani's eyes will help you better understand his spiritual greatness, whether you knew him or not. Narayani's own struggles—and growth—are also very interesting and enlightening. It was quite hard to put the book down once I began!"

–*Nayaswami Devarshi*, Director, Ananda Kriya Ministry, author

"A wonderful and charming account of a devotee's awakening to the spiritual path! Narayani lovingly served as Swami Kriyananda's personal assistant and caregiver during the last years of his life, and through her eyes we glimpse the greatness of Swamiji's spirit, his wisdom, and his all-embracing kindness. Her journey is ours and conveys what many of us have felt but have been unable to express."

–*Nayaswami Jaya*, Spiritual Codirector, Ananda India

"In this heart-stirring account of her years lived at the feet of a saint-in-the-making, Narayani offers the reader of her book both inspiration and lessons for the path toward enlightenment and inner freedom. I read from beginning to end in one sitting, moved both to tears and to out-loud laughter." –*Nayaswami Kirtani*, Spiritual Codirector, Ananda Europe

My Heart Remembers
SWAMI KRIYANANDA

My Heart Remembers
Swami Kriyananda

Narayani Anaya

CRYSTAL CLARITY PUBLISHERS Commerce, California

CRYSTAL CLARITY PUBLISHERS
crystalclarity.com | clarity@crystalclarity.com
1123 Goodrich Blvd. | Commerce, California
800.424.1055

ISBN   978-1-56589-055-8 (print)
ISBN   978-1-56589-513-3 (e-book)
Library of Congress Cataloging-in-Publication Data available

Cover and interior design by Tejindra Scott Tully

The *Joy Is Within You* symbol is registered by Ananda
Church of Self-Realization of Nevada County, California.

This book is dedicated to

My King

Special thanks to

Bryan McSweeney, Daya Taylor,
Lahari Palmer, Nirmala Schuppe, Andrea Roach,
Barbara Bingham, Tim and Lisa Clark,

**and many other wonderfully talented photographers,
known and unknown, who contributed
the loving images for this book.**

Contents

Foreword ~ 7

Acknowledgments ~ 10

Prologue ~ 13

What Is This Life? ~ 15

Welcome Home ~ 21

My King ~ 30

A New Tomorrow ~ 37

The Bhagavad Gita ~ 50

Aum Namo Narayana ~ 62

Portable Paradise ~ 73

From Jupiter to Earth ~ 87

The Nayaswami Order ~ 101

My Faith Is Tested ~ 111

My Faith Is Restored ~ 121

Learning to Walk ~ 133

Los Angeles ~ 145

Ever-New Bliss ~ 155

Everyone Is an Artist ~ 163

God Helping God ~ 177

You Will Need Help ~ 197

God's Call Within ~ 202

Moksha ~ 217

Door of My Heart ~ 231

Foreword

This is a unique book. Narayani played a very special role in the life of Swami Kriyananda, and she tells it here with love and clarity. If you accept, as I do, that we incarnate in each life with a special purpose, then you can see God's hand behind her story.

Most of Swami Kriyananda's close friends and co-workers came relatively early in his mission. He often told us, "Don't think about me as a personality, tune in to what I am trying to do. More importantly, tune in to how Master [Paramhansa Yogananda] is working through me." It is as if that first wave of people, destined to become the future leaders of Ananda, came in order to help Swami Kriyananda with his world mission. And he trained and empowered us for this purpose.

But as his body aged and became frail, he required a different kind of help. He needed someone who could tune in to his personal needs and help him to continue to help others. No dramatist could have written the role for Narayani nearly as well as the Divine Playwright. She came, relatively speaking, towards the end of Swamiji's life and mission. She came with almost none of the accumulated history, connections, and mission that defined many of the long-term members. She came not even knowing, at first, English, the language that was the carrier wave for Swami's vast thoughts, expressed through his books, lectures, and music.

This forced her to tune in solely to the vibration of his soul. With incredible persistence, she listened over and over to talks that she could not understand. But attuning to the tone of Swamiji's voice, and listening constantly to his music, she came to understand his consciousness with her heart and soul. That is the way of a true devotee.

When the time came for her to play her destined role as Swami's personal assistant, she was ready. Because of her deep attunement, she could anticipate his every need and help him play out his last years with grace and power, now expressed less through his thoughts, and more through his love for the Divine, for his guru, and for everyone who crossed his path.

This book is a wonderful window onto the later years in the life of a great saint. And it is a guidebook for how to attune oneself to the divine plan that guides each of us. As you read this book, do what she did: open your heart and soul, and you will find answers to many questions that live just below the surface of the mind and can be solved by love alone.

In divine friendship,

NAYASWAMI JYOTISH

Dharmacharya of Ananda Sangha

Acknowledgments

The process of writing this book has helped my heart also to remember the countless people who have made my life such a fulfilling adventure. I hope to find meaningful ways to personally acknowledge and thank each one of you.

Here let me mention just a few, without whom this book would not have been possible.

Jayashree Elena Poli, and Rohit and Rachna Sawhney, for giving me the time I needed to focus exclusively on writing. Asha Nayaswami for her invaluable help in editing, and most importantly, for encouraging me to tell my story confidently and fearlessly. And Shurjo Jha, my husband and best friend, for his total involvement in every aspect of this book.

Assisi, April 2013

One morning, I was trimming Swami's beard with electric clippers. He took my wrist and held my hand away from his face. The clippers continued to buzz as the background to the following exchange:

"Are you going to write a book about me?" he asked.

The thought had never crossed my mind. "I don't know," I said.

My first language is Spanish, so I raised the obvious objection. "My English isn't very good."

"Will it be a biography or reminiscences?" Swami asked.

"I would be more comfortable with reminiscences." Then I mentioned the language problem again.

"Don't worry. I will help you."

He let go of my wrist, I finished trimming his beard, and he never mentioned the book again.

Three weeks later, Swami passed from this world.

Five years old, 1984

What Is This Life?

A ll of my childhood memories are happy. My parents married young and I was the first-born, not only for them, but for my whole extended family in Elche, Spain. My grandfather sang flamenco. I had it in my blood, too, and from a young age loved to dance. My mother would set me on a tabletop, the family would clap the rhythm, and I would entertain them all.

I never wanted to dress in an ordinary way, but wrapped myself in colorful cloth and put flowers in my hair. I had to be a princess or a fairy. My brother was enough younger to be ordered around by his big sister. I made him wear costumes and practice dance steps with me so that, during carnival and the music festivals in town, we would look good together and have the right choreography. (He remembers these experiences less happily than I do!) I could never stand and watch but had to be in the procession, dancing through town.

My dad was interested in metaphysics, and says that when I was only four, I would ask him questions about karma and reincarnation. I remember watching a TV series about a young boy learning from a master, not only skills, but how to *live* in the right way. I was thrilled by the idea of having a Wise One to guide me.

As a small child, I would sleep in the far corner of my bed to leave room for all the angels who came to sleep with me. I trained myself not to move during the night, so I wouldn't roll over and crush any of them!

It made me sad to see poor people. I especially remember a family in our neighborhood with two children. I did what I could to help them. Whenever I cleaned up my room I would look for things to give away.

My father had to put aside his spiritual interests to build his career and raise a family. He was an interior designer and he and my mother opened a shop which became one of the most popular in Elche. She ran the store; he took care of the designs.

When my brother and I became teenagers, he became serious again—perhaps over-zealous—about yoga and meditation. He tried to get my mother to cook only vegetarian, something she couldn't imagine! She loved her life as it was, being a wife and mother, but a gap was opening between her and my father.

When I was fifteen, there was a bitter divorce.

My mother cried so much, especially at night, that I moved into her room and slept in her bed, hoping my presence would make her less sad and lonely.

It was all too much for me, more reality than I wanted to face, so I ran to the superficial side of life and had a few wild years.

My parents expected I would go to college, but when the time came I wasn't interested. I liked life and people, and didn't enjoy learning from books. After college you just had to get a job anyway, so what was the point?

I tried to think back to something that had made me happy before. I liked working with my hands. I remembered going to the beauty salon with my mother, then making the same styles on my dolls. Being a hairstylist did not fit my parents' expectations for me, but they agreed because at least that gave me some direction.

It turned out I had a talent for it. The all-female environment was a welcome change after my wilder years. When my teacher opened a shop, I went to work for her, and did very well. The relationship with my clients was about more than their hair; we connected on many levels.

I was earning enough money to take care of myself and work gave me more discipline. I still loved to dance, and every weekend I would go with my friends to the disco.

Life began to settle into a comfortable routine. I loved what I was doing, but couldn't imagine going on like this for the rest of my life! Husband and children were the obvious next step, but somehow I knew that wouldn't make me happy. The question was: *What would make me happy?*

I had no idea. Was this *all* there was to life?

My family, 1990

My Guru, Paramhansa Yogananda

Welcome Home

When my parents divorced, I stayed with my mother. Seeing how much she suffered, it was difficult to both support her and still remain open to my father. When I was young, I'd liked to talk to him about spiritual matters. Now his spirituality had been a factor in the break-up of my family, so I shut myself off, not only from him, but from that way of thinking about life.

When I started working and felt stronger in myself, I reestablished my relationship with my dad. When serious questions about the meaning of life began demanding answers, I knew he was the one who would understand and help me. He started giving me spiritual books, which I read at a rapid rate.

He had become a disciple of Paramhansa Yogananda and, when he felt it was appropriate, he handed me the book *Autobiography of a Yogi.* He thought I would like it, and he was right!

That book took me over completely! When my friends invited me out, I said no, without explaining that I had to stay home and read. I spent all my spare time with the *Autobiography.* Even at work, I kept my mind on the book, thinking about what I had read.

Autobiography of a Yogi introduced me to another reality. Everything I read was new and yet, at the same time, familiar. I started seeing my life in a way I had never done before: the quality of my energy, how it affected others; how their energy affected me; why I got along with some people while with others couldn't get along at all.

Suddenly I felt responsible for myself in a way I had never considered before. My life, from being boring and mediocre, had now become a great adventure — interesting, and with deep meaning behind it. I felt reborn.

When I came to the chapter where Yogananda meets his guru, Sri Yukteswar, I realized how much I, too, longed for a relationship like that. I knew without a doubt that I belonged to Yogananda.

I began looking for anything else written about

him. Unfortunately, there wasn't much in Spanish, the only language I knew at the time. My dad suggested I contact Self-Realization Fellowship and subscribe to Yogananda's lessons in meditation.

Each lesson covered a specific spiritual topic and also gave different meditation techniques. I loved these lessons, but they came only every two weeks. The time between the lessons felt like an eternity!

I learned to meditate, and got exposed to various aspects of Yogananda's teachings, but something was still missing. I wanted to feel Yogananda's vibrations more, and deeper. But *how*?

I'd been receiving these lessons for over a year when my dad called. "I've heard about a place called Ananda," he said. "The founder is Swami Kriyananda, one of Yogananda's direct disciples. They have a community in Assisi, Italy, and he is living there. I'm going to visit."

My dad spent two weeks at Ananda. He phoned as soon as he returned. "You must visit that community! Everyone felt like family. I met Swami Kriyananda briefly, and, I must say, he is something very special."

He was so enthusiastic about everything related to Ananda, he decided to open a small meditation center in Elche.

During his visit to Ananda Assisi, my dad met an American woman named Vairagi who had been living there for several years. Soon after, she was assigned to come to Spain to help him develop the meditation center. Vairagi spoke English, Italian, and Portuguese, but no Spanish. We spoke only Spanish. Still, somehow we were able to understand each other.

Whenever Vairagi came, she would talk to us about life at Ananda and discipleship to Yogananda. For the first time I was doing more than just *reading* about these teachings. Through Vairagi I was learning what it meant to *live* them.

She had been a member of Ananda for more than twenty-five years. Her life was dedicated to helping Swami Kriyananda spread Yogananda's message. Vairagi's commitment to the spiritual path made me love and respect her deeply. Every moment in her company brought me spiritual upliftment. She became my mentor; I wanted to be just like her.

In August 2002 I went with my dad to visit Ananda Assisi for the first time. The members of the community were from all over the world. Italian, English, and German were the main languages, none of which we spoke. Still, somehow, just as with Vairagi, we managed to communicate.

The main building is called *Il Rifugio* — The Refuge. It holds the reception, dining room, and kitchen. In the kitchen, the cooks prayed before preparing each meal, asking to be channels of God's love and joy, so others would feel those vibrations in the food. The meals were all vegetarian, and delicious!

What a revelation all this was for me! I too wanted to be a channel for God.

Temple of Light, Ananda Assisi

Every morning and evening, people would meditate and do yoga in the Temple of Light, a beautiful domed structure with a deep-blue tile roof. This trip was opening my mind to a new way of living. Until I came to

Ananda Assisi, I had never realized the *lack* of joy in my life, nor how deeply I *longed* for joy.

The way I had been living was so dry and meaningless compared to how people at Ananda lived. It was heaven on earth. I had found my home.

The day we arrived there was a concert in the Temple of Light. I was very curious about what kind of concert it would be. All I knew was that the music had been composed by Swami Kriyananda.

I am not a musician, but my parents liked music and there was often something playing at home — flamenco, the Beatles, Beethoven. On my own, I listened mostly to the popular singers in Spain, or something I could dance to at the disco.

In other words, I wasn't prepared for what my soul was about to experience.

After dinner, we went to the Temple, which was now set up with chairs. People were putting finishing touches on the altar. Most of the singers were gathered on the side, talking among themselves, passing music around, joking, laughing. The whole atmosphere was relaxed and happy.

The women were dressed modestly, with flowing skirts of beautiful colors. I saw instruments — violin, piano, cello, guitar — that gave me the impression this would be a refined kind of music.

Soon the director took over and invited the choir to the area in front of the altar. Graciously, without any fuss, they took their places. I saw Vairagi, and some people I had seen earlier cooking in the kitchen, now standing in the front. Also, Kirtani and Anand, leaders of the whole community, seemed happy being just two more in the choir. It seemed to make no difference who was who, or what positions they held. They were one united group.

Then they started to sing. Their voices were divine, as if a host of angels had just descended. Perfect harmony.

My mind, usually so restless, became suddenly still and quiet. I was fully in the present moment, here and now. My consciousness was lifted into a state of perfect love I had never experienced before, a love I didn't even know existed. With an explosion of tears, the floodgates of my heart opened.

An hour later, as the concert ended, Vairagi came over and hugged me. "I am not crying because I am sad," I told her. "I feel so much joy. This is all new for me."

The music had given back to me something I'd lost so long ago, I had almost forgotten it. But my heart remembered, and rejoiced to find it again.

People often ask me, "When did you first meet Swami Kriyananda?" Before I wrote this book, I would answer by recounting my first *physical* meeting with him. Now I realize my first meeting was that concert.

Swamiji often said, "If you want to know me, listen to my music."

My King

My second visit to Ananda Assisi was in March 2003. A group from Spain decided to go together for a special weekend dedicated to Paramhansa Yogananda. Swami Kriyananda would be there.

The program was held in a beautiful hotel in the town of Assisi. The lecture hall held about three hundred people. Our group of ten found places in the back. I could hardly see anything, but it didn't matter to me. I felt so lucky just to be attending my first talk by Swami Kriyananda, a direct disciple of Yogananda.

People had come from all over the world to attend this program. Swami was lecturing in Italian, and headphones were available for simultaneous translation. In the back of the hall, near where we were sitting, translators whispered into microphones in German, English, Spanish, Russian, and who knows how many other languages!

Swami's lecture, Assisi, 2003

When Swami began speaking, little by little, the outside world faded away. The people in the room, the whispered translations, the Spanish coming through my headphones — all disappeared. It was just me and *his* voice. It wasn't what the voice was saying, as I didn't understand most of it, but where his voice was taking me.

It was like the concert, only this time I wasn't confined to my own inner world. My consciousness expanded to embrace everything and everyone around me.

A sense of peace descended on me, deeper than any I had ever known.

By the time Swami finished his lecture, I was like a rock, absolutely still in my chair. Even as people around me began to move and talk, I stayed still and silent, hoping not to lose the peace that enveloped me.

After a few minutes, someone came over and said, "Your group is invited to have lunch with Swami Kriyananda."

The lunch included other visitors and residents of the community. It was a buffet; everyone served himself. I was walking toward the food table when suddenly I found myself standing in front of Swami. It was so unexpected that it took me a few seconds to realize it was *he*!

He smiled at me with shining eyes. I replied with a nervous smile of my own. No words were said, but at that moment everything shifted, and the thought flashed through my mind: "I am standing in front of a king: *my* king!" In my mind's eye, even his clothing changed into a royal robe and a crown. A noble ruler, not only of people and lands, but of *himself*. Master of his *inner* kingdom.

The day of the lecture happened also to be my twenty-forth birthday. When somebody brought a cake to our table, I thought, "Would it be presumptuous to go over to Swami's table and offer him a slice?" Presumptuous or not, I chose the most beautiful icing flower, put it on a piece of cake, and took it to him.

"Swamiji, today is my birthday. I wanted to share this piece of cake with you."

"Thank you," he said, as he accepted it graciously. "Unfortunately, I'm not allowed to eat sugar, but I will share this with my friends." Then he added, "But this flower, I will have."

A Spanish devotee had followed me with a video camera, making a film of the whole event for our friends in Spain. I asked Swamiji if he would say a few words into the camera for those who couldn't come.

In Spanish he said, "My Spanish isn't very good, but I hope to visit Spain sometime soon. I send my love to everyone there."

He then turned to me, placed his hand on my head, and wished me happy birthday.

At the time, I didn't understand the significance of that touch. Now I know that this is a way a master blesses and gives energy to his disciples. Swamiji's blessing was his birthday gift to me.

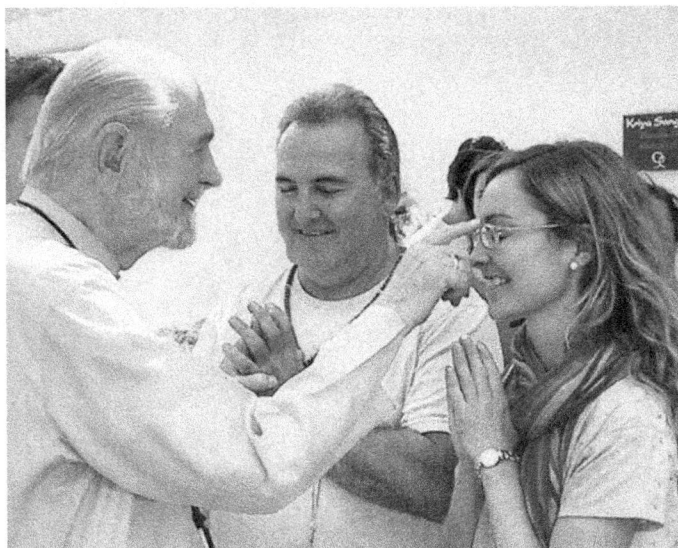

Swami blessing Dad and me

With Vairagi in India, 2005

A New Tomorrow

After meeting Swami Kriyananda and receiving his blessing on my birthday, my desire to grow spiritually became urgent. I loved being hairstylist, but I changed jobs and began working in a clothing store. I got the same pay for fewer hours, leaving me more time for my spiritual life.

I wanted to learn all about Swami. I read all the books I could find, although only a few books were in Spanish, so I had to use my dictionary. All I listened to now was Swami's music. He had recorded songs in English, Italian, Bengali, and Sanskrit. There were instrumental pieces, too. I listened to everything I could get my hands on!

I watched every video I could find and spent hours listening to his audio talks. Most were in English; some in Italian. I didn't understand very much, but that was not an obstacle for me. In fact, it was the sound and the vibration behind his words that I enjoyed the most. The barrier of language, rather than being my enemy, became my ally in getting to know Swami.

Day by day his vibration was transforming me. I was connecting with Swamiji on a level completely new to me, that I had never done with anyone before. I listened to Swami most of my waking hours. His voice resonated through my whole being, bringing peace to my soul. I was never alone, for he was my constant companion.

After months of listening to his talks in Italian (which was at least closer to Spanish than English), one day, suddenly, I could understand what he was saying! Not everything, but most of it. Now, I was able to connect his vibration to the stories and concepts he was sharing. It was a huge milestone.

I began to meditate on Swami: visualizing him, praying for him, and keeping my thoughts on him throughout the day. I kept up with all possible news of where he was and what he was doing in India, Italy, and America.

This not only helped me feel closer to Swamiji, it also intensified my yearning to feel God's presence within. I often prayed during that time, "God, help me grow spiritually as fast as possible. I want to burn as much karma as I can. Teach me to offer myself to You."

A few months after I started this prayer, I began to have severe headaches. My overall health deteriorated. In a short time, I lost a lot of weight. I went with my dad to see the doctor. After two days of intensive tests, we received the shocking results: thyroid cancer! The doctor said it was spreading fast and he needed to operate immediately to save my vocal cords.

The news shook us like an earthquake! My whole body started trembling.

I couldn't understand why this was happening to me. I was just twenty-four. The thought of dying at such a young age filled me with fear. The timing was the worst! I had finally found direction and meaning in life and was just starting on the spiritual path. Most importantly, I had found my Guru. Everything seemed right and good. But now, my world was falling apart. Why me? Why now? I must admit, my faith was shaken.

Then I saw my dad's face. I knew I had to draw on whatever strength I could, not only for myself, but for his sake and for my family's as well. I realized there had to be a lesson in this for me, and coming now meant that I was ready to learn it.

My dad and I hugged, and with tears flowing down our faces, said encouragingly to each other, "Everything will be all right."

I felt the blessing of having by my side not just a father, but a fellow disciple.

A week later, I made the connection between my fervent prayer to burn as much karma as I could, and the news of my cancer. This revelation completely changed my perspective. What I most needed now was to relax, trust, and accept God's will, whatever that might be.

My mantra became: God, Thy will be done.

I wrote Vairagi about the cancer. She answered immediately, "You should write Swamiji and ask him to pray for you."

"I don't want to tell him about this. It would only add an unnecessary worry for him," I said. But she was so insistent, I decided it certainly wouldn't hurt to have him praying for me.

I wrote Swamiji. Lakshman, his personal secretary, wrote back, requesting a picture so Swamiji could better visualize me when he prayed. Later that day, I received an email directly from Swamiji saying he would most certainly pray for me. He ended with these words: "I know God and Gurus are with you. They will give you the strength."

I put his email on my meditation altar to remind me that my Guru was always by my side. Swami's words became a protective force field around me that gave me the inner strength he promised. I was able to face the surgery as a warrior rather than a victim.

Day before surgery, 2004

The surgery went well. After a week in the hospital, I began to recover. I started eating and talking again without any problem. The harder part came later, with many months of chemo and radiotherapy. I knew it was just karma being burned and that it was only a matter of time. But that didn't make it any easier to bear.

Many nights my dad had to rush me to the hospital to make sure the pain I was experiencing was just part of the treatment process and nothing new had come up. It was a constant test of surrender, patience, and physical endurance.

I wrote Swami once a week to update him on my progress. In one of his emails back to me, he said, "Listen to my music. It will heal you."

I had been listening some, but now I went to sleep with his music and I woke up with his music. All day, every day, I listened over and over again.

Swami has often said, "All the music I have composed has been given to me. It is not my music; it is God's."

By attuning myself to his music, I was able to be with Swami on the level of consciousness from which he'd composed it. I know why I recovered so quickly:

because of the healing power of Swami's music. Just as he'd said.

I look back on this period as one of the most blessed of my life. My faith was tested and I came out the other end a better disciple. To offer my life fully into God's hands became the only reason for my existence. Now that God had saved my life, He had better take charge of it!

In April 2005, we received sad news. Vairagi had been diagnosed with cancer. Her life was coming to an end.

After she was diagnosed, she moved back to Ananda Village in California. Afraid that we might not see her again, my dad and I decided to visit her there. She wrote that instead of coming to California, we should meet her in India. She was going there to see Swami and to receive his blessings one last time.

When I first met Swami in March 2003, he was living in Assisi. A few months later he felt his guru's guidance to move to India. So with a small group of Ananda devotees he went there to start a work for Master.

Most of my treatments were over and I was feeling much stronger. So on May 14, we went to India. How excited I was! It was my first time in that country, but I had a strange feeling it would be very familiar to me. The moment my feet touched the ground, I felt a blessing descend upon me. I was home.

This turned out to be the most important trip of my life. It set the direction that I have followed ever since.

A taxi took us from the airport to our hotel in Gurgaon. Vairagi was in the lobby to greet us and I was overjoyed to see her again! Together we made the ten-minute walk to the ashram Swami had established in a beautiful neighborhood there.

When we arrived, we were shown around the ashram by some of the residents. Word came that Swamiji wanted to greet us later that afternoon at his house nearby. I had only been with Swami in a group setting. This would be a more intimate gathering than I had been in before. I had butterflies in my stomach!

At 4 p.m., our little group arrived at Swami's house. It was tastefully decorated in soft, warm colors; everything seemed to glow. The house was not luxurious, but to me, it felt like a palace.

Swamiji, dressed in his orange robes, sitting in a light-gold armchair, was waiting for us in the living room. The moment I saw him, my heart whispered, "*My King.*" I knew it had nothing to do with the clothes he wore or the house he lived in. He could have been sitting on a tiny wooden chair in a dingy little house, and he would still have appeared just as regal to me. "I am in the presence of royalty," I thought.

Swami stood up and greeted us with a radiant smile. I smiled back, but felt awkward in his majestic presence. In his role as host, Swami put us at ease in a matter of seconds.

In my subsequent years with him, I saw this happen time and again. Swami's ability to make even strangers feel like lifelong friends never ceased to amaze me. But this day I experienced it for the first time.

He asked about my health, then said, "I'm very happy to see you looking so well."

"It is all thanks to you, Swamiji."

He smiled. "Just God's grace."

We were together about an hour. The conversation was slow and simple, as three different languages were needed to make up for each other's limitations. It didn't matter; it wasn't about the conversation. I was where I belonged: with Swamiji. *He* was my home.

When it was time to say our goodbyes, Swamiji said, "I'd love to invite you out to dinner tomorrow. Would you be interested?"

Interested? We'd be *delighted*! It was much more than we could have imagined.

The next evening at 7 p.m. we went to Swami's house again. We were all decked out in new Indian outfits that we had bought that morning for this occasion. Seeing us in our shiny new clothes, Swami offered a few gracious compliments. When he looked at how I was wearing my *dupatta* — the Indian scarf that I had draped around my neck — he asked if he could show me another way to wear it.

Carefully Swamiji rearranged the dupatta around my shoulders. "There," he said, "that looks better on you."

Another woman in the group was wearing her dupatta the way I had had mine before. Just as she was about to rearrange hers, Swamiji said, "For you, that way is okay. No need to change."

Later, when I began to wear Indian clothes more often, I realized that this small outer adjustment also had an inner effect. I noticed a subtle positive difference in the way I felt and the energy I carried when I wore my dupatta as Swami suggested, compared to any other way of wearing it. Looking back on this incident, I also think Swami was testing me to see how open I would be to correction, even in front of other people.

The driver arrived with the car. Swami sat in the front and we all squeezed into the back. Before the car even left the driveway, Swamiji turned around, looked straight at me, and asked, "Would you like to live in India and help us with the work here?"

Dumbstruck by the question, I felt my face flush. Not quite sure what he meant, I stammered an answer, "W-w-w-well, let's see, Swamiji. W-w-why not?"

For the rest of the ride to the restaurant, I was mostly silent. My mind, though, was racing, trying to figure out what would happen if I accepted Swami's invitation and came to live in India. This trip, which had started as a simple visit to a friend, now, suddenly, could change my destiny forever.

We saw Swami a few more times, but only during his public events. He said nothing more about my possible move to India, until the very last day. We went over to his house to say our goodbyes. As I knelt before him, he blessed me, and with a twinkle in his eye said, "See you soon, right?"

I felt that a new life awaited me in my Guru's land. I was so happy! So eager! So grateful!

Our dinner together

The Bhagavad Gita

I made arrangements to go back to India as quickly as I could. I put in my notice at work and told the rest of my family. After consulting with my doctor, I bought my tickets for a three-month stay.

I landed in New Delhi on October 15, 2005. When I arrived at the Gurgaon ashram, I received the happy news that Swamiji wanted to welcome me.

As soon as I began to move towards his house, in my mind I was already with him. As I walked the now familiar route, I attuned my vibration to his, so that when I arrived there would be no transition.

Through the kitchen window, Swami's cook saw me coming. She opened the front door of what to me was both a temple and a palace. Swami was waiting for me in the living room. He took both my hands in his. "I wanted you to know how happy I am to have you with us."

Presenting the Gita to the late Indian president APJ Abdul Kalam, 2006

His words thrilled me. And at the same time the thought came: "Of course he would want me with him." Just as the father welcomed the prodigal son, I belonged to him.

To Swamiji I said, "I'm so happy to be with you."

Two weeks earlier, Swami had started working on the book *The Essence of the Bhagavad Gita Explained by Paramhansa Yogananda.*

"Please, come here anytime you want to read the manuscript," he said. Blessed with that invitation, and knowing I would be seeing Swami many, many times in the months to come, I left a few minutes later. What more could I ask for? My time in India was off to a fabulous start!

Finishing the Gita manuscript, 2005

I never doubted the rightness of being with Swami. Still, when I was away from him, I was often troubled by self-doubt. Not about my relationship with Swami, but about how I would fit into the work in India. The doubts came especially when I compared myself to others in the ashram, who had been with him for years, and seemed so competent.

When I arrived in India, many of the community leaders from around the world were also there visiting Swamiji. They took their meals at the ashram. When I saw them talking among themselves with a familiarity born of working so long together and with Swamiji, my self-doubt took over. I took my plate, sat down in a corner, and tried to make myself invisible.

It was a battle I had to fight for many years.

I asked one of Swami's staff for the best time to go read his manuscript. I wanted to be sure not to disturb him or force my presence on him.

Even years later, when I became his personal assistant, I was extremely careful never to intrude myself unless I knew it was what he wanted.

She suggested I go to read during his afternoon nap. That sounded perfect.

The next day I made my first attempt to read his commentary on a scripture I had never heard of, in a language I didn't know! When I arrived, two women from the ashram were already sitting, silently reading through the pages, passing them one to another.

I had come equipped with a small English-Spanish dictionary to help with the task before me. I sat down with the two women and one of them handed me the first pages. About fifteen minutes later, we heard Swami's voice and his footsteps as he came down the stairs. He greeted us happily, then joined us.

When he saw my little dictionary, he seemed surprised. "What do you need that for?"

I managed to convey to him that I wanted to understand what he had written; I didn't want to miss any part. I expected him to respond with some lighthearted comment. But in a serious manner, he said, "Don't worry, you'll be able to feel it."

His words were prophetic. Of course, even with the help of the dictionary, I wasn't able to understand word for word what he had written. But I found I was able to divine the essential message of each paragraph. When I held a page in my hand, I was transported by a powerful flow of energy into a higher realm of knowledge. Understanding did not manifest in the mind; it came as a feeling in the *heart*.

Swami was keen to get feedback from those who read his manuscript. He would thoughtfully consider each comment, no matter how big or small, and no matter from whom it came. Even from an inexperienced Spanish girl who needed a dictionary to get through each page! My comments sounded to me like the babbling of a two-year-old, but never once did Swami dismiss them as trivial or irrelevant. In fact, to one comment I made, he said, "That is a very good point. I'll add it."

He saw each and every one of us as a potential channel for Master. He was always open to any message Master might give him, through any person.

One afternoon, some of us were at Swami's house reading the pages he had written that day. He joined us, waiting patiently while we finished. People were passing pages one to another. As the slowest reader by far, I was the last in line.

Most people read a page in less than five minutes. I had to stop often to look a word up in my dictionary, so it would take me at least fifteen minutes. By the time the others finished and were ready to give feedback, I was still only halfway through. So sweetly, Swamiji asked them not to comment until I, too, was done.

One day I arranged to go to Swami's house in the evening to read. There were already two people there. The moment I sat on the sofa, Swamiji walked down the stairs and asked the three of us, as usual, which pages we were on.

He said, "Very good," and started walking into the main living room. At that moment the two people next to me started talking to each other. Swamiji turned back and said, "Don't talk now. Ana [my name then] needs to focus!"

Concentration had never been a strength of mine. I hadn't considered it that important until I began to meditate. That very morning I had prayed, "Master, help me to develop more concentration and focus in everything I do."

When I heard Swami use that word, focus, it took my breath away. Master had heard my prayer and was answering me through Swami. I knew then, more clearly than I had known before, that Master would use Swami to bring me closer to God.

One afternoon I was sitting at Swami's house reading that day's pages. When Swami greeted me from upstairs, I felt a particular quality of tenderness in his voice. When I saw him, he seemed to carry a subtle, feminine energy, different from anything I'd seen before.

Joyously he asked, with a phrase he often used, "And how are we today?"

"Very well. And you, Swamiji?"

He opened his arms wide, gazed upward, and with childlike glee said, "Divine Mother is flowing through me."

On another occasion, while busy with my reading, I suddenly became aware of a presence next to me. I looked over and, to my surprise, saw Swamiji sitting there in silence. *When did he come in? How long had he been there?* I couldn't say.

There was a halo of stillness surrounding him. I sat motionless, fearing that even the slightest movement on my part might disturb this feeling.

Then he asked me, "Do you like it?" meaning the page I was reading.

The question, though spoken aloud, didn't create a ripple in the ocean of stillness around us. "I love it, Swamiji." Now that the silence was broken, I added, "Swamiji, you feel different from the last time I saw you."

"I *am* different," he said. "I have just finished writing one of the most profound chapters of the Gita commentary."

During the time Swami was working on the Gita, I was amazed to see how, from day to day, he would manifest different aspects of the divine. Sometimes he was Stillness itself. Other times, the unconditional love of Divine Mother. On a different day it would be the ever-new bliss of God.

Little by little, my purpose for going to his house changed, from the study of the Gita to the study of Swami. I made it my practice to observe carefully every little thing he did. His gestures, expressions, interactions with others, the way he moved, the tone of his voice — all these became the object of my study. Eventually, I was able to perceive even the tiniest shifts in his energy, and knew what each meant in terms of his consciousness.

I didn't have any specific job in the ashram, but helped out wherever I was needed. About three weeks after I arrived, to my delight, I was asked to clean Swami's bedroom. To me, his whole house was a temple, and his bedroom, which I had never seen, was the sanctum sanctorum. When I entered for the first time, I felt so much reverence, I fell to my knees and placed my forehead on the carpet in *pronam.*

While vacuuming, dusting, and changing the sheets, I paid close attention to my thoughts. I knew Swamiji would feel the quality of energy I put into cleaning his room. I wanted him to feel my joy and gratitude for all he was doing for me. So I made it a point to chant or do *japa* throughout.

From then on, I went to Swami's house every week to clean his room. Before starting, I would pray to God and Guru to flow through me and fill his room with *Their* vibrations. I was helping Swami, but the beauty of it was, in putting out my best for him, it was I who was helped and transformed the most.

Swamiji gave many satsangs at the ashram during the months I was there, mostly about the Gita commentary he was writing. After one of them, a man said, "I was raised reading the Bhagavad Gita every night. But only now, after hearing you explain it, do I understand its true meaning. Every Indian must have your book in his home!"

"This is not my book," Swami said. "This is my Guru's book. It is his commentary, not mine. Master said about his interpretation of the Gita, 'Millions will find God through this book. I know. I have seen it.'"

Swamiji finished all six hundred pages of his Gita commentary in less than three months. The end of his work on the Gita coincided with the end of my stay in India.

Aum Namo Narayana

I returned to Spain in mid-December to spend Christmas with my family. I enjoyed being with them, but missed the daily Gita readings at Swami's house, the long meditations, the times of silence and solitude, and the growing friendships with people in the ashram. Being around Swamiji had changed me. After living in close proximity to someone with such high consciousness, I couldn't go back to the way I had been living before.

I had also come to Spain to see my doctor, to monitor the progress of my recovery. I had planned to return to India right away, but the doctor discovered a new growth of cells. Another treatment was needed.

I had just started reading the book *God Alone*, by Sister Gyanamata, Yogananda's most advanced woman disciple. She wrote about the inward relationship she

had with her guru. I felt the way she related to Master was the same way I related to Swamiji.

I wrote to Swami about what the doctor had found. I also shared with him the deep impact *God Alone* was having on me. Right after sending him that email, I went to meditate. Suddenly I felt Swamiji's presence, blessing me. "*He's reading my email and replying to me right now,*" I thought. I looked at my watch. It was 9:30 a.m.

After meditation I had to go right to the hospital so it wasn't until later in the evening that had a chance to check my emails. There was Swamiji's reply, sent at 9:30 a.m. The inward link that had been created during my time in India was still strong. No matter where I was, or how far away, Swamiji's blessings would reach me.

I had heard him say, "If you tune in to my consciousness, you can receive my thoughts." Now I knew it was true.

I wrote Swami often to keep him informed of my progress. It took me a full month to recover from this latest treatment. By then it was too late to see Swami in India. I was thrilled when he wrote to me, "I hope to see you in Assisi when I go there in the Spring." As soon as I got the green light from my doctor to travel, I went to Italy, arriving a few days before Swamiji.

The whole community was buzzing with excitement. It had been a year since his last visit. After a few days of rest, Swamiji decided to have lunch with the community.

Everyone lined up outside the dining room to greet him. When Kirtani saw me, she came over and said quietly, "Swamiji wants you to sit with him at his table."

"What?! Me sit at his table?" I asked her twice, "Are you sure?"

Swamiji was greeting everyone on his way to the dining room. When he saw me he smiled mischievously. "I'm glad you'll be sitting at my table. I hope you don't mind."

The place assigned to me was directly across from him. I thought, "Couldn't I just be at the end of the table? That way at least I could relax."

As much as I loved being in Swami's presence, I never had much to say, and what I did say always seemed inconsequential. I felt shy whenever I was with him, especially if other people were around. I found it easier to connect with Swami inwardly, and at a distance. Now, at his table with nine other people, I feared I would be expected to make intelligent conversation. *O Lord, please take me now!*

As lunch began, people came over to the table to greet Swamiji. While others at the table spoke softly among themselves, I sat silently, hoping to get through the lunch unnoticed. As if catching my thought, Swami looked across at me and said, "I'm so happy to have you here. When are you coming back to India?"

The moment he spoke to me, all my fears dissolved and I answered easily, "I don't know yet, Swamiji, but I hope to be there when you are there, too."

"Very good!" he replied. "That is the right thing for you."

Swamiji started talking to the whole table about his life in India and how much he felt at home there. Then he added with a smile, "But where I feel most at home is within myself. Center everywhere, circumference nowhere."

For the rest of the time, he shared stories of his life with his guru. Every story was a balanced mix of humor and spiritual depth. We were spellbound. I gained a new understanding of how Swami interacted with people. Whenever he spoke to someone, he looked directly into their eyes, transferring into them the experience he was describing. Everyone received equal attention. We were all living those memories with him.

What a marvelous host he was!

Even Swamiji's manners and etiquette at the table are worth mentioning. Every movement — even the act of eating — was deliberate and conscious. Nothing was mechanical or habit-based. The movement of his fingers, his way of sitting, his posture — everything was precise, but not strained. He was relaxed and at ease, engaged with everyone around him.

Whenever anyone came up to the table to greet him, Swamiji would stop eating, put his silverware aside, and focus completely on that person. He gave himself fully to every situation, whether it was buttering a piece of bread or greeting a friend.

Watching him at the table was beautiful and inspiring, like seeing a conductor lead an orchestra.

If this sounds exaggerated to you, it is because of my inability to convey the enormity of what I witnessed that day. For a moment, a veil had been lifted. I saw how a saint relates to the world around him and how he spiritualizes *everything* he does.

My first lunch with Swami was indeed very *full-feeling.*

I felt the effect of that time with Swami for the rest of my stay in Assisi. Everything I did was filled with his energy. Despite my body's weakness from the recent radiation therapy, I felt strong and energized. My meditations were deeper than they had ever been.

At the end of my first week, there was a Kriya Initiation. The day before, one of the community leaders, handed me an envelope with a rudraksha bracelet inside. She said, "I gave Swamiji a list of three names, asking him to whom I should give this bracelet. He blessed it and said I should give it to you, even though your name wasn't on the list."

I was so moved to realize that Swami was also thinking of me.

Kriya Initiation, 2006

Swami had given many people at Ananda spiritual names, usually Sanskrit. Taking a new name was a way to offer up your "old self" and affirm your aspiration to become a new and better person. A name might strengthen a quality you already had, or help you develop something you lacked. Swami would meditate and decide what was best for you.

Sometimes Swami received the inspiration for a name and offered it without being asked. Usually, though, you asked Swami for a name, and waited for him to meditate and decide what it should be. It could be a matter of days, weeks, months, or in some cases, years.

Sometimes people received their own inner guidance for a name and then asked Swami if he thought it was right. Or they might suggest several names and ask him to choose.

I thought a spiritual name could help me focus my energy and aspirations. Before I asked Swami, I wanted to be sure this desire was not merely egoic. Another thing that gave me pause was, I might receive a name I didn't like!

So I waited and meditated on it for the next few months. Only when I was ready to accept *any* outcome, would I ask for a name.

I wanted to learn to chant, so I borrowed a harmonium. Every evening I would play it in my room. I was a slow learner, but I enjoyed every bit of it.

One morning I woke up with Swami's chant "Aum Namo Narayana" playing in my head. It stayed with me throughout the day. When I got back to my room I thought, "I should learn it on the harmonium."

I found it in my music booklet and began to follow the notes. To my astonishment, my fingers flowed over the keys like never before. The chant took over without any effort on my part. I had never learned a chant so fast, or played it so well.

I chanted for hours. The energy rose up my spine and lodged in my heart. From there, I consciously lifted it to the spiritual eye, where it remained for the rest of the night.

◦◦◦ ◦◦◦

A week before my return to Spain, Swamiji again joined the community for lunch. This time I wasn't sitting at his table so I went to wish him farewell. "Swamiji, I'm leaving in a week and wanted to say goodbye. Thank you for all that you have done for me during this time in Assisi."

Swami was looking at me as I spoke, but I felt he was actually looking *through* me. Then, speaking to the whole table he said, "She looks like a daughter to me. I like her." Then coming back to the present reality, he said, "See you in India, right?"

Crystal Hermitage, Ananda Village

Portable Paradise

I returned to India in October 2006, this time for a six-month visit.

Housing at the ashram was an increasingly complicated situation. With more people joining and only a limited number of rooms, it was a constant juggling act. My first visit, I stayed in a tiny room that used to be the kitchen pantry. No windows. No door. I hung a piece of cloth over the entry to indicate that someone was now living there.

This time, once again, I was given my old "room." When the kitchen needed its pantry back, I was moved somewhere else. In that second move, my joyful attitude started to wane. By the fourth move, this time not just to a different room but to another house altogether, my joy completely disappeared.

I fell into one of those, "Why is this happening to me?" moods. I was plagued by such thoughts as: *People don't really care about me. They are not trying hard enough to find a place for me to live. Perhaps I shouldn't have come to India at all.* I began to cry, and just as my tears turned to sobs, my phone beeped. The whole ashram had been invited to watch a movie at Swami's house. My first thought was, "I'm not going!" I didn't want to put on a fake smile and pretend everything was fine. Because it wasn't! At the same time, I couldn't really turn down an invitation from Swami.

I wiped my tears, washed my face, pulled myself together as best I could, and marched over to Swami's house.

The room was full of cheerful, happy people. All, that is, except me. Hoping that Swami wouldn't see me, or sense my mood, I hid in the darkest corner I could find.

People were chatting among themselves as we waited for everyone to arrive. Suddenly, Swami, interrupting all conversation, said in a loud voice, "Master said, wherever we go, we should carry in our hearts a portable paradise. The sadhus in India make it a practice to move from one place to another every three days. I was thinking today how easily I could leave everything behind and never look back."

His words felt like a slap on my face — exactly what I needed to snap me out of my mood. This could have been a perfect opportunity to put the teachings into practice. Instead, I'd given in to self-pity. I let Swami's words sink deeply into me, and by the time the movie ended, my bad mood had completely disappeared.

I made the decision to accept my situation joyfully. Instead of feeling sorry for myself, I would build in my heart a portable paradise.

Of course, after I changed my attitude, I didn't have to move again. What's more, my new house was closer to Swami's. Just a two-minute walk away.

For a small group of Westerners, almost all new to India, trying to establish a work was not easy. It took every bit of everyone's time and energy, with nothing left over for relaxation. We shared a house, but everyone was so busy working on his or her project that we barely had any social interaction.

Cecilia Sharma, a devotee from Italy, came up with the idea of organizing a special brunch for the ashram residents, to which Swami would be invited. She asked for my help to make it happen. How we put the whole thing together is a story worth telling, but one I'll save for another time.

On January 5, we had a big public celebration for Master's birthday. The brunch was set for the day after.

In the back of my mind, all this time, I had been thinking about asking Swami for a spiritual name. After having meditated on it for months, I finally felt ready. So on the evening of Yogananda's birthday, I wrote to Swami.

The next morning, Cecilia and I went to the ashram to work on the final touches for the brunch. Through her inspired efforts, the dining room had been transformed into a five-star, pink and white extravaganza! It was delightful to see the pleased and amazed looks of the ashram residents as they entered the room. The intended effect had been achieved!

Everyone was relaxed and happy. The room was alive with conversation and laughter. After all the hard work of collecting nectar, the bees were finally enjoying some honey!

When Swamiji arrived, I watched from a distance as he walked around the room, admiring and complimenting everything: decorations, food, colors, flowers, and above all, the *spirit* he felt behind it all.

Then he asked, "Where is Ana?"

"I am here, Swamiji," I replied.

He motioned for me to come nearer to him. "I have something to tell you."

When I was standing in front of him, he said, "Last night, while meditating on your request, the name 'Narayani' came to me. I think it is perfect for you. It matches your energy." He touched me at the spiritual eye and blessed me in my new name.

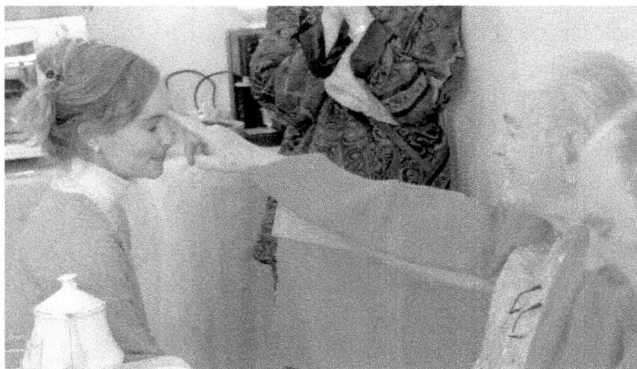

I had assumed it would be at least a few months before I received a name. It took me a few minutes to realize what had just happened. *Narayani!* My new name. I *loved* it! I felt baptized in the waters of Swami's love. I entered the room as Ana, and emerged as Narayani.

Swami told me that Narayani means "the feminine aspect of God."

Later that day, I remembered the connection I had felt the first time I played the chant "Aum Namo Narayana." The feeling I'd had then was the exact same feeling I had when Swami blessed me. Without realizing it, I had already tuned in to my spiritual name.

That night, I found my new name repeating in me, over and over again, as if to imprint itself on my consciousness. I felt as if a friendly virus had entered into me and was changing the old code of Ana into the new code of Narayani.

Ananda's work is primarily spread across three countries: the United States, Italy, and India. Each year, Swamiji spent a few months in each place. One day, while meditating, I received the sudden inspiration to follow Swami wherever he went. Like my desire for a spiritual name, I felt I needed to test this inspiration to make sure it was more than just a personal desire. I decided to wait and let the inspiration unfold on its own, rather than rush into it.

The guidance continued to intensify with each meditation, always accompanied by a calm, expansive feeling. Eventually, I decided to take the first step in that direction and see if the universe would support it.

I could have made the whole thing easier by asking Swamiji, but I knew that, for me, it was more important to develop and learn to trust my own intuition.

My first hurdle, which would pretty much prove my guidance true or false, was whether I could afford to do it. I had quit my job some time ago, and used up most of my savings visiting Swami in Assisi and India. When I told my father what I was feeling, he offered to support me. I knew he didn't have much money, so I hesitated to accept. But he insisted so much, I took it as a sign from the universe.

I am eternally grateful to my father, whose generosity and self-sacrifice made it possible for me to fulfill my destiny. With his help, work-exchange in the communities, and my skill as a hair stylist to make up the difference, my guidance became a reality.

For the next three years, I followed Swami from country to country. Wherever he was, I was there, too. When it came time for Swami to move on to the next place, he would ask if he would see me there as well. My answer was always, "Yes."

His answer was always, "Very good!"

Spiritually, those years were blissful. But on other levels, it wasn't always easy. Living out of a suitcase, accepting whatever accommodations were available, doing any job that was needed. Most of the time, seeing Swami was enough, but when waves of doubt or fear washed over me, Swami's "Very good!" was the raft to which I clung.

There are two separate properties at Ananda Village in California. The main community and the original, more remote land Swamiji bought in 1968, which is now Ananda Meditation Retreat. The two pieces are six miles apart.

When I went to Ananda Village, I decided to live at the Meditation Retreat. I thought going back to the place where it all started would help me attune myself, even more, to Swami.

My duties were to help in the kitchen and do house-keeping. I spent my free time deepening my spiritual practices: meditation, reading, listening to Swamiji's recorded talks (some of which had been given in this very place), doing japa, or just keeping silence. There were only a handful of us living there. It was blissful to be bathed in the stillness of the place.

Swamiji's residence, Crystal Hermitage, was at the Village, so I didn't see him as much as I had in India or Assisi, where everyone lived closer together. But every time he gave a talk or satsang, I was there.

I felt the inspiration to organize a special event at the Meditation Retreat that would be hosted by the youth of Ananda Village. Since it was on this very property that Swami, helped by a handful of others, had begun his work, I thought it would be especially meaningful if we, the next generation, could come together to express our gratitude.

By now I had met most of my generation living at the Village. When I shared this idea with them, their support and enthusiasm were overwhelming.

We divided up the responsibilities for the event. One group was in charge of the music and the concert, another was responsible for decorations and setup, and still another for the menu, cooking, and serving. We designed a lovely invitation card and sent it to all the community residents. The event began to generate a powerful energy of joy and inspiration that touched everyone who heard about it.

I sent a personal, handwritten invitation to Swamiji, to which he replied, "It would be my pleasure to attend."

After weeks of preparation and rehearsals, the day was finally upon us. Our group, all dressed up for the occasion, gathered together for a prayer before the event started.

When Swami arrived, we blessed the food. The feast and festivities officially began!

I went back to the kitchen to supervise Swami's meal, which had to be prepared in keeping with his dietary restrictions. There was a particular spice I knew he liked, so I went to the pantry to get it. It was on a shelf too high for me to reach, so I stood on a stool. Just as I was about to grab the spice, I slipped and fell. My right foot hit the floor with a loud *crack*! I tried to stand, but the pain was too much to bear. I had broken my foot!

More concerned about Swami receiving his food than about my foot, I asked someone to help me to the kitchen counter so I could finish his plate. Just then Swami walked into the kitchen. I was sitting with my foot on a chair, under an ice-pack.

Someone must have told him that I'd fallen, because he came straight to me and said, "This is one of the most inspiring events I've attended this summer. The energy is wonderful. I'm so sorry you had to pay the price of a broken foot."

"It has been worth it, Swamiji," I replied.

He smiled, then blessed me at the spiritual eye. Instantly, the intense pain disappeared and was replaced by an equally intense joy. Nothing else was said. Swamiji, still smiling, left the kitchen to go back to his seat and enjoy the rest of the program.

When it was time for the concert, I couldn't walk on my broken foot. Someone had to carry me to the stage, but when I was offered a chair, I chose to stand instead. For almost an hour, I balanced on one leg singing Swami's music. The pain was no longer an issue, but sometimes I couldn't sing because of the joy.

We ended the concert with one of Ananda's theme songs, "Many Hands Make a Miracle." Everyone stood up, applauding. Swamiji, with tears in his eyes, said, "Thank you, everyone. I'm deeply touched. I can see in you all the future of Ananda."

After the event, four hours since I had fallen, a friend drove me to the hospital where an x-ray confirmed that my foot was indeed broken.

The following weekend, Swami gave a satsang at Crystal Hermitage. I limped into his living room, on crutches, with my foot in a cast. From Swami there was no "Oh, poor you!" Instead, with a beautiful smile he said, "Look at you! A warrior! Never lose that inner strength."

Then he added, "You are coming to India, right?"

I was set to leave for Spain in a week, and then on to India. I approached Swami after the satsang to receive his blessing.

He said, "It takes courage to bring people together in harmony. That is what Master likes. I'm so glad to see you doing that."

Lunch at Tonino's, Gurgaon, 2008

From Jupiter to Earth

I spent almost two months in Spain, waiting for my broken foot to heal before I went to India.

From the time Swami moved to India in 2003, his hope had always been to buy land to build a temple, a headquarters, and a community. He looked all around Delhi and Gurgaon, but nothing worked out.

In 2008, one of our devotees found thirty acres on the outskirts of Pune, a city 1500 kilometers south of Delhi. A group from the ashram went to see it and came back with positive reviews. One thing led to another and, by the end of the year, we purchased the property, hoping to build there our first community in India. It was located in the tiny village of Watunde, in the foothills of the Shivalik mountain range, an hour-and-a-half drive from Pune city. It was raw land, with absolutely nothing on it.

An advance party from Gurgaon moved to Pune to prepare the way for Swami's eventual move. The first step was to build basic infrastructure: roads, electricity, water. Then came the matter of housing, especially for Swamiji, whose presence would be vital in magnetizing a community there.

In the meantime, the group moved into rented apartments in Pune. On the weekends, they gave classes in meditation and Kriya Yoga to build an awareness of Ananda's presence. Almost every day during the week, they went to the land to help get the project, literally, "off the ground."

For those still in Gurgaon, there was a certain amount of tension. The ashram residents were mostly Americans and Europeans who had come to build the work in India. They were committed to the project, whatever it took, but had also hoped to do that work living close to Swami.

Now he was leaving for a city far away, and, obviously, not everyone could go with him. The work in Gurgaon also had to continue. Who would go with Swami? Who would stay behind?

I, too, agonized over this for a few weeks. Uncharacteristically for me, I finally decided just to ask

Pioneers, Ananda Pune, 2009

Swami what I should do. "I think it will be good for you to go to Pune," he said. So in January 2009, I moved with Swami and his staff to Pune city.

I shared a three-bedroom apartment with two other devotees. As part of my *seva*, I cooked meals for Swamiji's staff. I also helped his personal cook with the washing up after meals. I was so happy to be of some use.

Soon after we arrived in Pune, Swamiji started recording an audiobook of *The New Path*, his auto-biography. One of the apartments was converted into a makeshift studio. We were all invited to listen to

Swamiji record. It took two months of almost daily sessions to finish the book.

I had read *The New Path* before, but hearing Swami read it was an entirely different experience. It was like having a personal conversation with him about the most important events of his life.

Like a sponge, I absorbed as much as I could. I paid close attention not only to what he was saying but to his tone as he expressed it. I began to see how certain tones related to certain emotions and states of consciousness. Sometimes I would get so lost in the vibration of his voice, I would forget that the words had any meaning.

Every morning I would go to the recording studio ten minutes before the session started, to make sure Swamiji had a glass of water and a box of tissues next to him. The recording engineer closed and *locked* the door precisely at 10 a.m. If you were late, you couldn't get in. So I was careful always to be on time because I never, *ever*, wanted to miss even one of his sessions!

I usually served lunch at 1:30 p.m. Since the recording often lasted till 1:00 p.m., I had to plan carefully to have everything ready on time. I would prepare things the evening before so I only needed to heat it up the next day.

One evening, Swamiji invited me and a few others to go out to dinner with him. We arrived home too late for me to prepare the next day's food. "Oh well," I thought, "I'll get up early and do it in the morning." Unfortunately, instead of waking up early, I woke up much later than usual: just forty-five minutes before the session was due to begin.

I rushed to the kitchen and worked as fast as I could, but by the time I was done it was already 10 a.m. I ran up the stairs as I've never run before, only to find the door locked. I was five minutes too late! I was devastated. I couldn't bear the thought that on the other side of that door Swamiji was talking and I wasn't there to hear him. I sat on the floor and leaned against the wall, trying my best not to cry.

Then, to my astonishment, the door of the studio opened and Swamiji walked out! "I don't feel like recording this morning," he said to me. "I'll try again this afternoon." As he was stepping into the elevator he added, "Be sure to make it this time."

These recording sessions, though wonderful for us, put a strain on Swamiji's health. He had to talk for hours every day, staring at the pages on a computer screen. With each passing day, you could see the toll this was taking on him. I wondered, "Is there something I could do to help him?" The thought came of offering him a head massage.

I mentioned my thought to one of Swami's staff members and asked her to ask him. It would be easier that way for him to say no. A few days passed with no answer, so I asked someone else to ask him. That person said, "If Swamiji wants a head rub, he will ask for it." So I let go of the idea.

But the following day, after the afternoon session, he told us how heavy his head felt because of the effort he was putting out. I *had* to do something to help him, but was too shy to speak in front of so many people.

When Swamiji stood to leave, a few of us followed him into the hall. As he stepped into the elevator, he looked right at me and said, "Would you like to come in?" When the doors closed I felt an unseen force pushing me to speak. "Swamiji, would a head massage help? If so, I'd be happy to give you one. Or someone else could."

"I'd love for you to do it," he said. "Are you free now? My head feels really heavy."

I was nervous because I'd never given a head massage to anyone before. I mentally prayed, "Master, use me as your channel." When I placed my hands on Swamiji's head I felt heat emanating from it. I closed my eyes, visualized Master, then felt my hands being intuitively guided. Bit by bit, the heat from Swami's head diminished.

After fifteen minutes, he said, "Thank you very much! That's enough for now."

The way he said it made me feel that perhaps he didn't like it. But then he added, "That was one of the best head rubs I've ever had. Could you please come again tomorrow? I would very much appreciate it."

"Absolutely, Swamiji!"

From that day on, I was drawn closer into Swami's circle. Thinking of him as the Sun, I moved from the orbit of Jupiter to the orbit of Earth. I began to see him often in more informal settings: going out for coffee, meals, shopping, movies at his apartment. Gradually, I started relaxing more in his presence and soon lost my shyness and was able to express myself to him.

For the next four years I gave Swamiji a head massage almost every day. I wasn't always able to open myself as fully as I did that first time, but I tried my best.

Yogananda said that in a previous life he had been William the Conqueror, and that many of those close to him in this life had been with him then. Swamiji felt that he had been William's son, Henry I.

A member of Ananda, Catherine Kairavi, spent years researching the lives of William and Henry, looking for similarities with Yogananda and Kriyananda. She wrote a book about what she discovered, titled *Two Souls, Four Lives*, which Swamiji was now editing. The subject was so interesting that in every conversation he would share stories about these two kings.

Fascinated by the whole subject, I started doing research of my own. I got so involved, I felt I was living more in that period of history than the present one! Intuitively I knew *I had been with Swami in that lifetime.* I wrote him to say how familiar that period felt to me.

He replied, "Maybe you were one of my daughters when I was Henry."

Reading that email took me back to Assisi, when Swami had said, "She feels like a daughter to me." And even further back, to my first impression of Swamiji as "my king." All the threads were weaving together; the tapestry was revealing itself.

Yogananda also said that he had been a king in Spain. He didn't say which king, only that he had helped drive the Moors from the country. Naturally we were all curious as to who he might have been. Someone from Ananda researched the question and suggested two possibilities: King Alfonso VIII or King Ferdinand III, who was known as *The Saint*.

Swamiji asked me to look into it. "Try to tune in to their personalities and feel which one resonates with Master's."

That night I looked for everything I could find about these two kings: their lives, families, children, hobbies — anything that could give me a hint. After hours of research, I felt Ferdinand III was the more similar to Master.

Next morning when I saw Swamiji, the first thing he asked was if I had found anything interesting. "From all that I've read," I told him, "it seems likely that Master was Ferdinand III. In his own lifetime, people called him The Saint. Later he was canonized by the Church. His tomb is in the Cathedral of Seville, where to this day his body remains incorrupt. The tomb is open to the public one day a year, May 30."

"I would love to go there!" Swami said.

Now that we were inclined to think that Ferdinand III was Master, the obvious next question was, who was Swami? Ferdinand's son, Alfonso X, known as *The Wise*, was a good possibility. We had many lively discussions speculating about this.

Swamiji wrote in an email:

> I've been thinking. Master wrote of Sri Yukteswar that he was like a warrior; had been a warrior. I don't remember the exact words, but they are in the *Autobiography*. Could Alfonso VIII, Fernando III, and Alfonso X have been Sri Yukteswar, Master, and myself? An intriguing thought, and a resolution to the question of whether Master was Alfonso VIII or Fernando III.

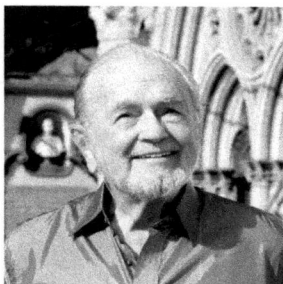

I now focused my research on Alfonso X, as Swami was eager to know more about him. An interesting fact was that Alfonso X was an extremely generous king, an unusual quality for that time in history. He cared deeply for everyone around him and liked to give to the poor. I sent this new information to Swamiji and received this reply:

How very interesting, about Alfonso X. I remember my father once scolding me: "You've just *got* to stop giving all your money away!" I think you know I didn't let him buy me a tuxedo when I was sixteen, as I "would never earn enough money to pay income tax!"

Who was his successor? Could you have been my granddaughter then?! I'm very much looking forward to learning more about Alfonso X. Fascinating.

In our discussions about the Spanish kings, Swamiji often repeated his desire to go to Seville and visit Ferdinand's tomb. He wanted to feel for himself if Ferdinand was indeed Master.

My time in India was coming to an end; in two weeks I would return to Spain. A small group of us went out to dinner with Swami. He talked about his upcoming holiday in Lugano, Switzerland, describing what a lovely place it is. Then he said to me, "I think you'd enjoy Lugano. Would you like to come?"

Unsure of what to say, I replied, "Thank you, Swami. It would be nice, but let's see."

That evening, back in my room, I thought of how much a trip like this would cost. I certainly didn't have the money, but if this was meant to be, the universe would conspire to make it happen.

There were also other factors to consider. Swami never went on holiday alone. Always some of his old friends went with him, usually the directors of Ananda's various communities. I wondered how I would fit in, and how they would feel about having me around.

After that, each time Swami saw me he would ask, "Any further thoughts about Lugano?"

My answer was always the same, "I'm working on it, Swamiji."

A few days before my scheduled departure, my friend Lahari invited me to her house for tea. Soon after I arrived, she handed me an envelope. "I can see how much Swamiji wants you to join him in Lugano," she said. "I would like to help make this happen. Take this as a gift from Divine Mother."

In the envelope was enough money to cover at least half the cost of the trip. The universe, through her, was cooperating.

When I went to say my goodbyes to Swamiji, again he asked about Lugano. Confidently this time I said, "YES! I'll be there."

With a big smile, Swamiji said, "That's my girl!"

The Nayaswami Order

I went first to Spain, for medical checkups and to see my family, then on to Rome to meet Swami and his friends. Together we drove to Lugano.

I spent most of the drive in silence, feeling like the odd one out. I had never been on holiday with Swami, or spent much time with this group of his longtime friends. I was extremely nervous and hadn't the first clue whom I should talk to or what I should say. Swamiji and the others were in one hotel. Miriam, Swami's nurse, and I shared a room in a less expensive hotel next door. I had gotten to know Miriam in India and felt comfortable with her. I made her my guide and followed her every move.

Just before leaving India, Swami had had a serious health crisis. For a time we thought he wouldn't be able to travel, but in the end he decided to come to Europe as planned. Once in Lugano, he began to feel a little better.

I had the opportunity to observe Swami in a new setting, watching his interactions with his friends and the way he related uniquely to each one.

On our second day, Swami talked about creating a new monastic order that wouldn't distinguish between married or single — where *everyone* could dedicate his or her life to God. He didn't say much beyond that, only that he had been thinking about this for years.

On the last day, Swami had another serious health crisis. The doctor Miriam consulted wanted to put him in the hospital, but Swami decided it would be better to go home to Assisi. A request was sent out to Ananda members everywhere to pray for Swamiji.

By the time we got home, Swamiji could hardly walk. I remember how he collapsed onto the bed.

Later that afternoon, I received word that Swamiji wanted me to give him a head rub. I went to his house around 8:00 p.m. I knocked, but there was no answer so I entered quietly. Swami was lying on the couch. He didn't have the strength even to greet me. When I went up to him, he opened his eyes and said, "I don't know what is wrong with me. I wonder if I'll live through this."

Hoping my positive energy would help him, I said, "Of course you'll get through this, Swamiji. You still have a great work to do."

"Only if Master wants it," he replied.

Not wanting to burden him with any unnecessary chatter, I began massaging his head. I prayed as I have never prayed before, asking Master to infuse Swami with healing energy. After forty-five minutes, I left the house, still worried. *What was going on? What could be paralyzing Swami's energy like this?*

I spent most of the night praying for him.

The following day, Swamiji's energy miraculously returned. He felt Master had restored his health so that he could start the new monastic order.

The traditional understanding of renunciation, Swami said, was out of sync with the times. We are moving now from fixed forms and ideas to an expansive new age of energy awareness. Renunciation is for everyone, married or single, who sincerely seeks to dissolve his or her ego identity. That very day he began writing the book *A Renunciate Order for the New Age*.

Taking the brahmacharya vow

For centuries, the traditional swami color has been orange. For the Nayaswami Order — "*naya*" means new — Swami changed the color to blue. Orange represents fire burning up all that a swami renounces. Blue is the color of the Christ consciousness — what a swami aspires to realize. By changing the color, Swami was changing the focus of renunciation itself, from world-*negating* to bliss-*affirming*.

What was remarkable to me was how *confidently* Swamiji changed centuries of tradition. No fear, no hesitation. He felt Master guiding him, and that was all that mattered.

The very next day, he put aside his orange robes. From then on he wore blue.

This was such an important moment in Swami's life. I was eager to be part of it. Taking *brahmacharya* vows, however, was no light decision. My call to monasticism had always been strong, and now the Nayaswami Order could give me a way to express it. *What if I failed to live up to the vows? What if my feelings changed in the future?* I was filled with doubts and fears.

To me these vows were meant to be lifelong. The very thought of breaking them frightened me. If I were to take the vow, I wanted to do it with the right attitude. In meditation I offered up my doubts and fears to Master and Swamiji, and surrendered myself to their will.

Finally I came to the conclusion that I needn't worry about the future. All that mattered was NOW, and right now, I knew this vow was the next step in my relationship with God.

Swamiji led the first Nayaswami Initiation on November 20, 2009, in Assisi. Many longtime Ananda members came from around the world to be initiated. I can't recall a more powerful ceremony. I took the *brahmacharya* vow.

RENUNCIATE VOW
of BRAHMACHARYA

I understand, and fully accept, that the true purpose of
life for all human beings is to seek God.

In pursuit of that goal, I offer my own life
unreservedly to seeking my Divine Source.

I will retain no ego-gratifying goal in my life,
but will strive always, and above all, to please God.

I will look upon life as God's dream-drama,
and also dream-entertainment. I will accept as
His gift whatever comes to me in life.

I renounce attachment to things, people, places,
and all self-definitions — except one: I will define myself always as a child of God, and will obey
whatever guidance He gives me.

I offer to Thee, Lord, my life, my desires,
my attachments, and the fruit of all my labors.

Bless me, and strengthen me, that I become
ever more perfect in this, my holy vow.

A few days after the initiation, Swamiji sent this email to Ananda members worldwide:

> We had our first nayaswami initiation last Friday evening, November 20. There were fifty-four people who took vows: twenty-two nayaswamis, and the rest into brahm-acharya, tyagya, and a few postulants. It was a memorable and moving ceremony. . . .
>
> A new era has been launched, not only for Ananda, but for people everywhere who want to declare their devotion to high, spiritual ideals.

Please give us your blessings. For me, personally, this event marks the culmination of many years of meditation and thinking.

love, swami

The power generated by the Nayaswami Initiation carried us, blissfully, into the Christmas season. This was the first time in many years Swamiji had spent Christmas in Assisi. The community was thrilled.

For Christmas Eve dinner, to my great joy, Kirtani invited me to sit at Swami's table. Usually, when Swami was there, the whole hall mirrored his lively energy. But that evening he was in a still and inward mood. Even when interacting with others, he emanated a quality of stillness, as if celebrating Christmas inwardly, at the Christ center.

When I expressed my gratitude to Kirtani for placing me at Swami's table, she said, "Swamiji wanted to be with close friends that evening and he said you were one of them."

After dinner there was a concert. When Swamiji entered the Temple to take his seat, I heard him call out, "Where is Narayani?"

"I'm here, Swamiji," I called from my usual place in the back row. Pointing to the empty chair next to him he said, "Please come and sit next to me."

The choir performed Swami's oratorio, *Christ Lives.* It describes the life of Christ, his teachings, death, and resurrection. For the hour-and-a-half performance, I sat perfectly still with eyes closed, trying to feel what Swami was feeling as he listened to that divine music. I visualized a golden cord connecting my spiritual eye to his.

His consciousness felt like a vast ocean, spreading out in all directions. And I, a little drop, was one with that ocean.

Swami was scheduled to return to India right after Christmas. I flew back with him, ready for another six months of spiritual adventure, hot weather — and *samosas*!

Pune community, 2010

My Faith Is Tested

We were still living at the apartments in Pune city, but work on Swami's house on the new property was in full swing. India, however, has its own set of rules when it comes to the concept of time. In keeping with that tradition, the house was taking longer to finish than expected. Fortunately, Swamiji's scheduled vacation to Goa bought us two more weeks.

Still, we weren't very optimistic about having the house ready in time. Something always came up: from a last minute change in the price, to workers not showing up because someone's grandmother had died (for the fourth time that month!).

Every morning a group of men from the ashram drove to the property to help with the building. As the only girl, and now a brahmacharini, it wasn't always easy finding an appropriate place to fit in. But one way or another I made that trip every day. I was determined to do everything I could to have Swami's house ready for his return.

The situation wasn't encouraging: unpainted walls, holes where there ought to have been windows, no water, electricity, or plumbing. On top of that, the hired crew, who should have been working at *top speed*, rarely arrived before 11:00 a.m. What we needed was a miracle!

The first task I set myself was to clear away the mess around the outside of his house — construction debris, rocks, bricks, clothes, bottles, tobacco pouches, wrappers, and all kinds of other junk. Then, when the workers finally showed up, I would grab a paint brush and work alongside of them, hoping to shame them into increasing their speed.

Even though *much* remained to be done, a few days before Swami's arrival we decided to move his furniture and belongings into the new house. I was asked to supervise this move. We hired a professional moving company, and on the appointed day a half dozen laborers descended on his apartment. Unable to communicate with them, I resorted to hand gestures to make myself understood. Since the workers were spread all over the apartment, I ran from room to room to make sure nothing was broken or stolen. It was absolute chaos. At last, however, we got everything packed and loaded onto the truck.

The driveway to the new house was steep and unpaved. As hard as they tried, they couldn't get the moving truck closer than fifty meters, which meant even more work. Once we got everything inside, I had to open each box, checking things off the list, to make sure nothing was broken or missing, before the laborers could finally leave.

One serious problem still remained. The contractors had promised us, before the move, that the windows would be in, but — guess what? — they weren't!

It was unthinkable to leave Swami's things unguarded, so for the next few days the monks took turns being night watchman.

By the time Swamiji returned from Goa the house was *almost* liveable. In an effort to make it more homey — and to distract Swami from all that still needed to be done — a friend and I got up early that morning to hang all the curtains. Just as we put the last curtain on his bedroom window, we heard people outside shouting, "Swami is here!"

Swami was delighted to see the house so close to ready. He wanted to move in right away.

A few other houses were also livable, but not much else was ready. Not wanting to be away from Swamiji, I borrowed a small tent and made it my home for the next five months. Life was rustic, with most basic amenities still lacking. I shared a bathroom with the construction workers. Water, when we had any, was a beautiful brown color. Meals were simple — sometimes rice and dal; sometimes dal and rice.

I loved it. My soul rejoiced in this spirit of renunciation.

A special weekend event was planned for Yogananda's Mahasamadhi. Our hope was to have people come and experience life at the community. There was only one tiny problem: we had no place for them to stay! We sprang into action. A flat section of the property was cleared to create a campsite where we could pitch some tents. We also converted three storage rooms into dormitories.

One of my responsibilities was to transform those storage rooms into living quarters. This meant redoing the floors, painting the walls, ordering the beds, buying mattresses, sheets, towels, quilts, and anything else that would make our guests feel comfortable. We also put up a makeshift temple using bamboo and straw.

A hundred people came that weekend to hear Swamiji talk about Master. About forty of them stayed the night.

Swami's house, Pune, 2010

Soon after Swamiji moved to the land, he began working on a children's book called *The Time Tunnel*. It was about two brothers and their adventures as they travelled through time, visiting different periods of history. Most afternoons, Swami would invite me over for tea and to read what he had written that day. It was delightful, in the midst of my dusty, construction-filled life, to escape for a time into a world of fun, joy, and adventure.

While talking about Ferdinand III and Alfonso X one afternoon, Swamiji again expressed a desire to visit Ferdinand's tomb in Spain. "Perhaps you could organize a trip for me," he said. "I could also do a public event. What about a book launch of the Spanish edition of *Autobiography of a Yogi*?"

Me?! Organize something on that scale?

Fear and doubt set in almost instantly. But what followed was the *knowing* that Swami would never ask of me anything that wasn't for my own good. Saying "yes" to his requests in the past had always brought huge blessings in my life. So I put aside my fears and vowed to make this trip a reality.

He made this request in February. Ferdinand's tomb opened only on May 30. That gave me three months to put the whole thing together. I wouldn't be back in

Spain until the end of April, so I had to organize most of it from India! Every time Swami saw me, all he would talk about was the exciting trip to Seville ahead of us.

Often Swamiji asked me to give him a head rub, either in the afternoon, or to come back later in the evening. I was grateful for the opportunity to give back to him. He was doing so much for all of us. I only wish I could have given him more.

One afternoon Swami said to me, "Please come, not only for tea, but as often as you can. Your presence brings peace to my environment."

After that, I began spending more time in Swami's house. The two of us would sit quietly in his living room, perhaps he with his book and I with mine. Sometimes I would tidy up, or organize his shelves, or do anything I could to uplift his environment, always making sure that my energy was in tune with his flow.

One evening, Swamiji had had a particularly demanding day. He wasn't feeling well and asked me to give him a head rub. I did my best, but apparently he still had a bad night.

Someone who heard about it was convinced that my head rub — and perhaps my very presence in Swami's life — rather than being of benefit to him, was the *cause* of his distress. With great force she declared to me, "The only reason Swamiji asks you to come over is to help you. But in giving you so much energy he is draining himself. You should stop following Swamiji around and settle down in one of the communities!"

For some minutes she went on in this way while I stared at her in total silence. To say I was stunned doesn't begin to describe the earthquake her words set off inside me! Yes, Swamiji had invited me, and seemed even to welcome me, but perhaps I had misunderstood him completely! I so wanted to be of help to Swami that maybe I had imagined it all! She had been with him longer and would know better than I. Even if Swami was willing to sacrifice himself for me, I couldn't let him to do that.

When she finally stopped, I assured her my *only* intention was to help Swamiji. I promised he would not have to suffer anymore because of me. Never again would I put him in a situation where he felt he *needed* to give me energy.

I tried to be brave, but my heart was shattered. I ran to my tent and cried until I had no more tears. I stayed inside the tent all day, desperately trying to reconcile what I felt from Swamiji and what he himself had *said* to me, with what this person was saying.

When the time came to go to Swami's house to give him another head rub, I didn't go. I couldn't! If this was only about him giving energy to *me*, I didn't want it! My only purpose was to give to him. I thought I had understood Swamiji, but now I didn't know what was true.

Next day, still inwardly grieving, I tried to go about my daily seva as if nothing had happened. When Swamiji invited me for tea, I couldn't say no. As soon as I walked in, in a worried voice he said, "Why didn't you come last evening? I was expecting you."

I was in too much turmoil to explain, so I simply said, "I'm sorry. I wasn't feeling well."

Inwardly, though, I had resolved: I would no longer impose my presence on Swamiji. After Seville, my time with him was done.

My Faith Is Restored

I arrived in Elche, then flew to Seville to finalize the plans for Swami's visit. Since this might be my last time with him, I wanted to be doubly sure this this trip would be everything he could hope for. I went straight to the Cathedral where Ferdinand's body was kept. From India, I had been in touch with Margarita, the coordinator of the Cathedral. I had explained to her who Swamiji was, his interest in Ferdinand's life, and his present health condition. I hoped she would assist us on the day of the opening.

Knowing how difficult it was for Swami to walk even short distances, the next item on my agenda was to rent a wheelchair. After that, hiring an English-speaking guide for all the historical monuments we would visit, finding a few restaurants with good vegetarian options, and walking the streets looking for anything that might interest Swami.

I wanted to offer this trip to Swamiji as a gift from the Ananda devotees in Spain. I had written them from Pune, asking if they would like to contribute towards this gift. Many sent money, but it wasn't enough. A year earlier I had sold my apartment in Spain so I could afford to continue traveling with Swami. Since this could be my last trip with him, I thought to use the remaining money to make up the difference between what I had raised and what the trip would cost.

I asked my dad for his advice. "It's your money," he said, "do whatever you feel is best. But when that money is gone, that's it! There won't be any more."

I decided there was no better use for my money than in service to Swamiji. I put everything that was left of my savings into his trip.

On the day of Swamiji's arrival, I went to the airport to welcome him, but his flight was several hours late. When the plane finally landed, I expected to see a very tired Swami. Instead, he practically ran towards me at the arrivals gate. Taking both my hands in his, he repeated, in carefully rehearsed Spanish, *"No por mucho madrugar amanece mas temprano."* Which roughly translates to, "Not by waking up early will the sun rise earlier!" We both burst out laughing because this was exactly what happened to him. He got up very early to catch the flight but arrived very late.

Miriam and some friends from Assisi accompanied Swamiji on this trip. I had booked us rooms in Seville's best hotel — Hotel Alfonso XIII. At dinner, all Swamiji could talk about was how eager he was to visit the tomb, and to see if the vibrations of Ferdinand's body felt like Master.

Early the next morning — May 30 — we put Swamiji in the wheelchair and together went to the Cathedral, which was a short walk from the hotel. There was already a long queue of people. I called Margarita to see if there was anything she could do. A few minutes later she was leading us past the crowd, right to the tomb. Swamiji was being escorted for his own private audience with King Ferdinand III.

Ferdinand's tomb

When we reached the tomb, out of respect for the saint who lay before him, Swamiji stood up from his wheelchair. I felt a wave of reverence and devotion descend over him. We sat to meditate on the benches in front of the tomb.

During meditation, Swamiji got up and walked as close as he could to where the body lay. I helped him climb a few steps, then continued to stand behind him in case he needed assistance. For several years, Swamiji had had trouble standing for long periods of time. But today, for over twenty minutes, he stood absolutely motionless, with his eyes closed, seemingly unaware of the weight of his own body. Then he sat back down and meditated for ten minutes more.

He stood up and reverently pronamed. We all followed suit, then silently made our way to the exit. We were eager to hear what Swami had felt inside, but none of us wanted to disturb his deep stillness. A whole hour passed before Swamiji spoke. "This is a powerful place. I felt it was Master."

For the rest of the day Swamiji remained withdrawn from all that was going on around him. It wasn't until the evening that he was fully with us again.

The next day we took a horse carriage tour of the city. "I have been here before," he said to me. "This feels like home. Doesn't it seem familiar to you?"

"Yes, Swamiji. It does."

That afternoon, we went on a boat ride with all the devotees from Europe and America who had come to be part of Swamiji's public event. I was sitting next to Swamiji when he said, "I feel past-life memories coming to me." After that, he withdrew into himself and remained silent for the rest of the ride.

The launch of the Spanish edition of *Autobiography of a Yogi* was deep, powerful, and life-changing for the many who came. Swamiji lectured almost entirely in Spanish. He had asked me to help with the translation, but he hardly needed it.

Throughout the trip, I spent all day, every day, with Swami, coordinating his activities and making sure he had everything he needed.

If I never had another time with him, these memories would feed me for the rest of my life.

"This has been one of the best trips of my life," Swami told me on our last day. "I hope we will have many more like it."

As happy as I was that Swamiji enjoyed himself so much, his words "many more like it" reawoke the sadness in my heart.

Swamiji flew back to Rome, where he was scheduled for another book launch. This time the Italian edition of *Religion in the New Age*. That very day he sent me this email:

Carissima Narayani,

Thank you again and again for all the loving energy you put into making this weekend such a glowing success. To me also, you behaved so dearly that I cannot but feel we have been very close to one another in other lives — and in how many of them? Thank you for all your love and kindness to me.

The visit to Fernando III's tomb; to Alfonso X's treasure room; the trip by horse carriage through Sevilla; the truly elegant hotel; the restaurants and outings: all these things and many more will remain warm and loving memories in my heart for the rest of my life.

I look forward to seeing you this weekend in Rome.

love, swami

P.S. I think what we all accomplished in Spain on this visit will bring lasting benefits for your country.

A few days later I flew to Rome to attend the event, and make arrangements to settle down in our Assisi community, as that woman had told me I must. Looking back I don't know why I allowed her point of view to influence me so strongly, but it did.

I was staying at the same hotel as Swami. When I arrived, he was standing outside. "I've been waiting for you. I'm so glad you are here. Come, let's have some lunch."

Swamiji kept me next to him throughout the weekend. He spoke about visiting Los Angeles in the summer and seemed to assume I would be there too. I had hoped to tell him my intention of moving permanently to the Assisi community. Now, with him talking about future plans that included me, I needed to do so as soon as possible.

A special dinner had been arranged for Swamiji and a few others. I was invited, but decided to stay in my room and meditate on the best way to tell Swamiji my plans. My phone rang. It was one of Swami's dinner companions. "Narayani, Swamiji keeps asking why you are not here. He would like you to come."

When I got to the restaurant, Swami said, "There she is! I was looking for you." Making space next to him at the table, he said, "Please bring a chair and join us."

After dinner, a small group of us walked Swamiji to the door of his room. "Narayani, would you mind coming in for a moment to help me with something?"

We walked in and he sat down on a chair. "Could you please bring me that book there, and my reading glasses?" Assuming this simple request was just a prelude to the reason he asked me to come in, I waited quietly for a few moments. When no further request followed, I asked, "Is there anything else, Swamiji?"

"No, that's it. Thank you. Good night."

As I left his room I thought, "Very soon Swami will need someone full-time to help him."

Helping Swami in this way was the most natural thing for me. Yet here I was planning to do the exact opposite. My mind was in turmoil.

That night I told Master in meditation, "Tomorrow I'm going to tell Swamiji my plans. If I'm wrong you have to let me know — very clearly."

The next morning Swamiji invited a few of us to join him for breakfast. We met first in his room.

"I've been thinking how helpful it has been having Narayani around," Swami said. "And the older I get, the more help I seem to be needing. Perhaps she could be my personal assistant and travel with us, as part of the staff."

Swamiji had addressed his remarks to the whole group, but seemed interested now only in what I had to say. "What do you think, Narayani?"

"I don't know if I'm worthy of this honor, Swamiji, but I would love it!"

"I know many people would like to serve me," Swami said, addressing the group again, "but they all have other responsibilities. I need someone whose only responsibility is to help me. I think Narayani would be perfect. Don't you all agree?"

Then to me he said, "Don't worry about your expenses. Ananda will take care of it. Wherever I go, you'll be with me."

I'd never told Swami or anyone else that I had spent all my savings on the trip to Seville. I stood silent and amazed at how *clearly* Master had answered my prayer.

I resolved from this point forward, in my relationship with Swami, to always trust my heart.

Months later Swami told me that when he was standing at Ferdinand's tomb in Seville, he asked Master, "Is it right to have Narayani close to me?"

"I received an instant blessing," Swami said.

In the Bible, Jesus says, "And everyone that hath forsaken houses, or brethren, or sisters, or father, or mother, or wife, or children, or lands for my name's sake, shall receive a hundred-fold, and shall inherit everlasting life."

That's exactly how I felt, except I was receiving a *thousand*fold!

Learning to Walk

The following day we drove from Rome to Assisi. It was my first official day as Swamiji's personal assistant, so when we got to his house, I went in with him. I needed to learn how things were done. Watching and helping Miriam was an ideal way to begin.

When Swami was ready for his nap, I headed for the door. "Could you please come back at 4:00 and help me take a walk?" He said, "It is important for my health that I exercise, but it is hard to do on my own."

"Of course, Swamiji."

When I returned at 4:00 p.m. I found Swamiji "awake and ready" for his walk. "Could you please help me with my sandals?" he said.

In India, touching the feet of a saint is a common gesture of respect, as well as a way to receive the saint's blessings. I saw many devotees, and even strangers on the street, touch Swamiji's feet, especially when he was dressed in his orange robes. But I had never touched his feet before.

I remember every little detail of that moment: the softness of his skin, the shape of his foot, the position of his toes. Carefully I put his sandals on, afraid I might hurt him. "Very good," he said. "Let's go."

I opened the door to let him out, then closed it behind us. Unsure of the protocol for my role as assistant, I waited for Swamiji to make the first move. He slipped his arm into mine, and with a gentle nudge, signaled me forward.

For Swamiji walking was already a bit of a challenge. When he linked his arm with mine, he also leaned into me so I could shoulder some of his weight. We walked for thrity minutes, up and back his long, quiet driveway, forested on both sides with tall trees. He hardly spoke, which was good, as most of my attention went into supporting him, matching my pace to his, and even trying to match the rhythm of his breath. All this helped me subtly attune to his consciousness.

In *The New Path*, Swami shares his experience of walking arm in arm with Master, shouldering his weight as the Guru was "drunk with ecstasy."

That first day with Swamiji felt the same to me as it had been for Swami with Master.

Back home, I again helped Swamiji with his sandals. He had an appointment for 5:00 p.m. and asked me to come back at 8:00 p.m.

On my way back to where I was staying, I noticed how exhausted I was. This was strange, because usually after being with Swami I felt energized. *If a simple walk had this effect on me, how could I be of much use to him?*

Since my first meeting with Swamiji I had watched him closely, observing his physical gestures, mannerisms, and expressions for what they revealed to me about his consciousness. Now something entirely new was being asked of me: to observe his body for the sake of his body. Food, sleep, exercise—things I hadn't given much thought to before—were now also part of my responsibility.

As his personal assistant I would now have to be equally attentive to all aspects of his being, human and divine.

In our daily walks I learned to attune to the dynamics of his physical body: the strength required to carry his weight; when he was tired and needed to stop; when to push a little to help him walk more. I became sensitive to the meaning behind the different kinds of pressure I felt from Swami through our linked arms. Tuning myself to his physical needs helped me attune better, also, to his consciousness. Each side helped the other.

I remember one humorous incident that happened when I was still learning the ropes around Swamiji. We were in Assisi, and he was scheduled to give an afternoon satsang at the Temple. In the middle of his talk he started sneezing. I knew any moment he was going to ask for a Kleenex, and I wanted to be ready. I asked those around me if anyone had one, but to no avail.

Just then, as I'd expected, Swamiji said "Could I please have a Kleenex?"

I ran to the bathroom, grabbed a generous amount of toilet paper, folded it into several neat layers, went back to the Temple and handed it to Swamiji. I was glowing with pride over my quick response to his need. Before he could use it, though, the neat folds came undone and the long ribbon of paper rolled open, reaching all the way to his feet.

In humorous surprise, holding the paper up by the corner, he exclaimed, "And what is this?"

Everyone in the Temple burst out laughing. Setting the toilet paper aside, he said imploringly, "Could someone please give me some proper Kleenex?"

I was so embarrassed, I turned red as a tomato!

I've mentioned before my trouble with shyness, and concern about other people's opinion of me. In front of all these people, I had to face that weakness once again. First, I had experienced pride over my "solution-oriented" thinking. Then intense shyness and embarrassment when my "solution" proved a disaster instead.

It is common practice to associate pride with ego. Shyness is usually brushed off as something harmless. In both cases, however, there is equal identification with ego. Whether you are being praised or pitied, both force a person to dwell too much on himself, drawing focus to the "I."

With my pride and shyness now on equal footing, the need to overcome my shyness became obvious. I couldn't brush it aside anymore. Swamiji, through this little episode, highlighted for me the need to speed up the process.

The other obvious lesson: *Always carry Kleenex.*

Writing about sneezing brings another totally un-related story to mind. This was much later in my time with Swamiji. By then, he was having trouble with his balance and was in constant danger of tripping or fall-ing. He couldn't even walk around the house without someone assisting him. I had to be with him pretty much all the time.

As if that weren't enough, Swamiji was also suffering from insomnia. This meant that I, too, didn't get much sleep. Our days were hectic, perhaps one of the busiest periods of my time with him. It amazed me, with all that was going on, and with so little sleep, the amount of en-ergy he could still express throughout the day.

I wasn't even close to his level! Many mornings I woke up with the thought: *If only I could sleep a little longer!* But of course, I wanted to help Swami and that thought got me right out of bed.

One morning, while helping him get dressed, I started sneezing. First one, then another, and another. I couldn't stop. I thought to myself, "This is great! If I'm sick, I'll be able to get some sleep!"

Picking up my thought, Swami said, "Can't you just use your will power?" There was a kind of strength in his voice that left me almost paralyzed.

I barely muttered a response, "I'll try, Swamiji."

Then, more sweetly, he said, "The power of the mind can overcome anything."

Suddenly, all feeling of tiredness disappeared. Even the *thought* of wanting to rest vanished. Swamiji wanted me to understand the importance of *not allowing my negative thoughts to influence my energy.* Especially to watch out for the attitudes of "I need . . .", "I can't . . .", or "I don't want to."

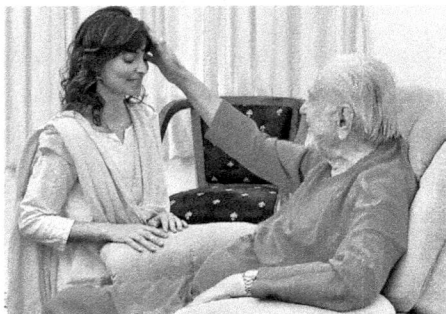

It soon became obvious that I needed to work on my English. I could understand almost everything, but I was unable to express myself fully. I remember early in my service to Swamiji he remarked jokingly, "I didn't know your English was so terrible!"

After that realization, Swamiji made it his mission to help me improve. He came up with the idea that I should write him an email every night, describing any event or story that I wanted. He would then correct my grammar, mark my mistakes, and send it back to me.

I started sending him trivial stories or descriptions of my day. As if he didn't already have enough to do! Sixty years of discipleship to an *avatar*, his great wisdom and exalted state of consciousness, all culminating in teaching English to a Spanish girl! Poor Swami!

"You could be doing so many more important things," I would often implore him.

"Don't forget to write your email tonight. I will be waiting," was his only reply.

This is one he sent back to me:

> *Dear Narayani:*
>
> Here are a few little mistakes you made that I'll correct here:
>
> 1. "Refermator": should be <u>Reformer</u>.
>
> 2. "Protecciton": should be <u>protection</u>.
>
> 3. "in all levels": should be <u>on</u> all levels.
>
> 4. "loose the game": should be <u>lose</u> the game.
>
> 5. "cualities": should be <u>qualities</u>.
>
> Other little things, but your letter shows definite improvement. Keep up the good work!
>
> *love, swami*

With each email, I made slow but steady progress. In the midst of this, I had to go back to Spain for a few weeks to renew my visa. Swami and I decided to take a break from my daily assignments, but I promised to still write him as much as I could.

To one of my emails from Spain, he replied, "Oh no! Please, come back soon, your Spanish is ruining your English!"

At times, he would tell others, "She is from Spain. I'm trying to teach her English, but she has such a thick accent!"

Even though this process was a lot of fun, Swamiji was *very* serious about what we were doing and at times reminded me strongly that this was *not* a laughing matter. He once wrote me:

> Now, Narayani, I have a serious request to make of you: Please make a special effort to study English. You will be able to serve this work in so many good ways, but if you know English your ability to do so will be increased a thousandfold. Your English is a little like my Spanish! Well, maybe much better, but . . . !
>
> *Much love to you, and many blessings.*

I can't claim to have been a good student, but clearly Swamiji was a good teacher, because here I am (with a little help from my friends), writing this book in English!

Ford Amphitheatre, Los Angeles, 2010

Los Angeles

was on Swami's staff now. So in the spring, when he left Italy for America, I went with him. For a few months we lived at Ananda Village, then moved to Los Angeles. Swami had recently sent several Ananda leaders there to start a center. Now he felt he should add his energy to theirs.

Master had called Los Angeles the "Benares of the West," and established his headquarters, and most of his Self-Realization Fellowship churches, in that area. More disciples of Master lived in Southern California than in any other area in the world.

Swami had been part of SRF for fourteen years, eventually becoming vice-president. But in 1962, the president, Daya Mata, became convinced that Swami could not be trusted and expelled him.

It was the most difficult test Swami ever faced. Eventually he started Ananda and began to serve Master in his own way. Daya Mata, however, to the end of her life, continued to undermine his work and discredit him as a disciple, including filing a massive lawsuit that took twelve years to resolve.

It was a deep pain for Swami that someone he loved as a spiritual sister could treat him in such an unkind way. "Can't she feel my consciousness?" he said to me. "Can't she see what a good work we are doing for Master?"

Just before we moved to Los Angeles, Swami started writing a book he called *Yogananda for the World*. It was about SRF, Ananda, Daya Mata, and the future of Master's work. He knew it would create controversy but time was running out and he had to speak frankly.

Most of those close to Swami were by his side through many years of SRF's opposition, including the lawsuit. I had come later, so my only connection was through Swami. And my only concern was to help him do whatever he needed to face what was unresolved, and to remove from his heart whatever pain he still carried.

As soon as he started writing the book, he felt an intense pain in his back, like someone stabbing him with a knife. The pain stayed with him until the book was finished. Sometimes, when he was typing at the computer, I would stand behind him massaging his back for an hour or more. He felt the pain was a force trying to stop him, and he wouldn't be stopped.

Starting then, and the whole time we were in Los Angeles, I felt the forces of light and darkness doing battle around us.

Swami didn't have his own home in Los Angeles, so one of our members invited him to stay with her. He moved into the guest house on her property. Swami had asked Jyotish and Devi, Spiritual Directors of Ananda Worldwide, to come help him establish the center. So the two of them, three others of Swami's staff, our generous host, her two daughters, and I all lived in the main house. It was pretty crowded! In the beginning I slept in a hallway, and later on a mattress on the floor of Miriam's room.

Swami began to draw me very close. There had always been certain respectful boundaries around him, which he himself supported. No one just "dropped in" on Swami. You went when you had an invitation or a duty to perform. Now Swami made it clear that he wanted me to be with him whenever I could, all the time if possible.

He asked me to come meditate with him every morning. I continued to sleep in the main house, except for those nights when I didn't feel it was safe to leave Swamiji alone. Then I would lie down on the couch in his living room. Otherwise, I tried to do as he asked, and spent all my time with him.

Soon he turned over to me almost all decisions about his personal and private schedule. He gave me the responsibility and also the intuition I needed to carry it out. I was able to know what he would want without having to ask him. Questions he used to answer himself, he now referred to me. There was no formal announcement, but soon it was obvious that this was what he wanted.

All his life, Swami had taken karma on his body, for the benefit of the work and to help others. Now he was having terrible insomnia. Many nights I was awake with him for hours. When he took a nap, he asked me to stay in his house so that when he woke up I would be there. He said I was a protection for him.

One night, as I was helping get Swami ready for bed, I felt a strange energy in the house. Like a dark, heavy cloud. When I mentioned it, Swami said he felt it too. "There is a constant war going on between light and darkness in the astral plane. I think that is what we are feeling."

I decided I shouldn't leave him alone, and went to sleep in the living room. In the middle of the night I heard a loud thud, then Swami calling my name. I found him on the floor, next to the bed. Fortunately, nothing was broken, but he had a nasty bruise on his right arm.

"What happened?" I asked.

"I'm not sure," Swami said. "But I felt something push me onto the floor. I think Satan is trying to stop me from what I came here to do."

The struggle wasn't only about Master's work. Swami's consciousness was changing. Giving me the responsibility for his outer life gave him more freedom to soar into higher states of inner bliss. It was a delicate transition, though, in ways I couldn't quite understand.

Swami would sometimes talk to me about the pain he still carried in his heart about Daya Mata. Her continued antagonism toward him, he felt, was hurting her spiritually. Both of them were coming to the end of their lives, and he wanted to help her if he could. That's why he was writing the book.

Swami moved to Los Angeles in August. At the end of November he finished writing *Yogananda for the World*. Within a day or two Daya Mata died. Swami wrote a personal note of condolence to the SRF members. A friend took me to SRF headquarters to deliver his note, and a big bouquet of flowers, to a specific senior monk he knew there.

When I walked into the SRF building, I felt my vibration merge with Swami's. I was *his* messenger delivering *his* consciousness of pure love for Daya Mata. No regret. No sadness. No animosity. Only love.

Soon after, we went to Hawaii for a month and the intense insomnia began to go away. He had a crisis with a blood clot in his leg and he couldn't fly, so we had to stay several more weeks.

When we finally returned to Los Angeles, it felt like a new chapter.

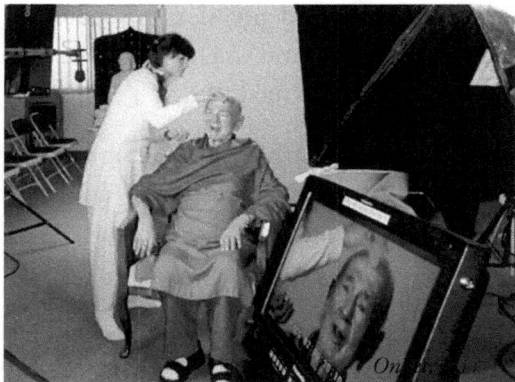

Swami was very busy working on a movie about Ananda, doing radio interviews, writing a series of lessons about how to achieve success spiritually and materially. He had me with him in every situation, public and private. From being a shy person in the background, I was now right next to him, making decisions and speaking for him.

Whenever I was with Swami, which was nearly all the time now, I had to watch my energy very carefully to be sure it was high and pure. I didn't want to bring anything of myself into the picture. I had to constantly match his refined and elevated vibration.

I had thought that meditation and personal sadhana were the way to make spiritual progress. Now especially, with Swami so busy and not sleeping much, I didn't have time for sadhana. And when I did, I was usually so exhausted it was hard to meditate.

I had to rearrange my thinking. Taking care of Swami was my sadhana now. Even basic needs, like sleep, or eating properly, or having a room of my own — all these priorities had to change.

Swamiji was expanding into bliss and Master wanted me, in my small way, to expand with him.

Ananda Los Angeles, 2010

Ever-New Bliss

e moved to Ananda Village in the summer of 2011. To make it easier for me to take care of Swami, the office down the hall from his private living quarters was converted into a bedroom for me.

Shortly after our arrival there, Swami began experiencing pain in his chest so severe it was hard for him to breathe. Many nights he was unable to sleep.

"I feel as if I am suffocating," he said. We tried several different things, including supplemental oxygen, but nothing gave any lasting relief.

Many nights I stayed awake with him, mostly meditating and praying for God to give him respite. Finally, out of sheer exhaustion, around 4 or 5 in the morning, he would fall asleep.

During one of those sleepless nights he told me, "I believe my heart is changing and that is why I have this pain. My love for God is getting deeper and deeper. I feel so close to Him."

I understood then that the source of his pain was not physical. I began paying even closer attention to Swamiji, to see if I could also tune in to this inward shift. I noticed how sensitive he had become to the feelings and experiences of others, as if there was no separation between him and the people nearby.

I recall one day, a man and his wife, longtime Ananda members, came to talk to Swami. For years they had been trying to find their place in the community. The couple felt increasingly isolated and misunderstood. The leaders had done their best to help them, but nothing seemed to come together, partly because the couple didn't always cooperate in a way that would have made things work.

To Swamiji, though, it didn't matter who was at fault. The couple were suffering intensely and his only concern was to help ease their pain.

I can still picture the scene as clearly today as when it happened.

Swamiji was in his chair in the living room and the couple sat facing him. At a certain point, as they narrated their side of the story, I saw Swami's consciousness suddenly shift. The couple seemed to feel it too and fell silent.

Swamiji reached out to them. As he held their hands, they moved from their chairs to kneel at his feet. After so many years of feeling misunderstood, they surrendered gratefully into his compassion and love.

Tears poured down their cheeks. As they wept, Swamiji wept with them.

Later Swami called the community leaders. "I know there are two sides to every story. You have tried in your way, and they have tried in theirs. Right now, though, our only concern is to help them heal their pain."

One afternoon, Swamiji lay down for a nap, but was unable to sleep. I thought watching a movie might help him to relax. He chose to watch *The Song of Bernadette*. This is the story of a young French girl from Lourdes who had visitations from the Virgin Mary. Many miracles were performed through that contact, but still people did not believe her. She faced much ridicule and opposition.

Eventually, Bernadette entered a convent. There, as a novice nun, she was mistreated by her superiors and faced many hardships. When we came to that scene in the movie, Swamiji began to cry. I had seen his eyes fill with tears during sensitive scenes in other movies, but this was like no other. He cried as if he himself were going through what Bernadette was experiencing: her suffering, the injustice of it all.

"Please, let's stop the movie," he said. "I can't watch any more. The pain I feel in my heart is too much to bear."

He cried, he said, not only for Bernadette, but also for the superior and what she would suffer because of her ignorance. And for all those who have embraced a monastic life, but are ignorant of — or, far worse, *indifferent* to — God's all-embracing love.

He was silent for a moment, then said quietly, "Because of the intensity of my feelings now, it is difficult to have a normal life. I feel so much bliss, I often find myself crying at the very thought of God's Love."

Then, after a pause, he added, "Please don't share this with anyone yet. People won't understand."

The mere mention of his guru's name, a kind gesture, a song, a beautiful sunset, would fill him with overwhelming bliss. Often, in the middle of a lecture, he would be unable to speak because of the intensity of his feelings. "I am so embarrassed when I cry in front of other people," he told me, "but the bliss is so strong I can't help myself."

I began to notice the little patterns that were linked to his inner states. Small movements of his body, facial expressions, or changes in the color of his skin often signaled an oncoming rush of bliss. Once I learned to recognize these signs, I was always careful during those moments not to disturb him. If we were in the middle of a conversation, I would instantly go silent, even leave the room if I felt he wanted to be alone.

Often when that bliss came to him in the presence of others, I felt Swamiji expand his bubble of bliss to include everyone. It wasn't really *his* bliss. It was God's bliss flowing through him. And, as he often told us, "It is the nature of bliss to want to expand itself."

Towards the end of Swami's life it became harder and harder to distinguish between him and his guru.

Swamiji was melting into God, and Master was the bridge.

He would say, "I no longer know where Kriyananda ends and Yogananda begins."

Writing the biography

In 2012, Swami began writing a new book: *Paramhansa Yogananda: A Biography*. One morning I found him lying in bed, eyes open, staring at the ceiling. He was perfectly still, yet I felt the room vibrating with energy.

"Last night I woke up at 3:00 a.m., and wrote an entire chapter about Kriya Yoga. Would you please go to my computer and read it."

When I came back after reading the chapter he was still staring at the ceiling. But now I noticed something I had missed before: his eyes! They were shining with an intensity I'd never seen before. His whole face was aglow — not normal, considering he had been awake most of the night.

With a divine smile and that extraordinary light in his eyes, he asked, "How did you like the chapter?"

"It is so powerful!" I said.

"Really? What did I write? I haven't read it myself yet. I awoke with a flow of inspiration that took me into another state of consciousness. Words were just given to me. I always feel Master's consciousness in whatever I do, but last night, it was Master himself."

Then, as if feeling the need to come back to this earthly plane, he said, "I'm hungry! Ready for a good breakfast?"

Everyone Is an Artist

In his book *Art as a Hidden Message: A Guide to Self-Realization*, Swamiji writes that the true purpose of art, in all its forms, is to uplift man's consciousness. Whenever he saw artists who wanted to use their art to inspire others, he supported and encouraged them.

With some friends from Assisi, we were on holiday one time in Sorrento, Italy. While walking through the streets one afternoon, a beautiful painting caught Swamiji's eye. It was a young mother bending down to kiss her child. The painting exquisitely captured the subtlety of the mother's emotions.

Eagerly he entered the shop. He stared deeply at the mother and child. "There is so much love in this painting," he said, as tears filled his eyes. Turning to our friends, Narya and Laura, he said, "I want to buy this painting for you as a gift."

To the shopkeeper he said, "I would like to thank the artist personally for his sensitivity. Do you know how to reach him?" But all the shopkeeper knew was that the artist's name was Raffaele Concilio and about once a month he came to collect his earnings and deliver new paintings. So Swamiji asked Narya to see if he could find him.

It took Narya a month to locate the artist. When Swami finally had the address, he wrote him this letter:

Dear Raffaele:

I am an American. I know Italian, but when I want to be perfectly clear I write in English and hope the recipient either knows enough English to understand me, or knows someone who can translate my letter for me.

I was in Sorrento recently, and bought two of your really excellent paintings. One of them you were kind enough to sign, of a young mother kissing her baby. The other one you had just brought in that day.

Really, sir, you are an extraordinary artist! I know of no one who can capture the human countenance so well as you do.

I myself am the founder of several communities in the world, including one near Assisi. I am also the composer of more than 400 pieces of music — songs and instrumentals — and part of my mission in life has been to bring people the joy of God. I have, besides, written and published some 150 books, and have also written poems and plays.

Part of my mission in life is to sponsor uplifting self-expression in all the arts. Your painting of that mother shows such sensitivity that I would like to encourage you to make it at least part of your mission to bring inspiration, and not only beauty, to people.

For example:

1. A painting showing the joy in a penitent's eyes after making his confession.

2. A priest speaking in church, with the light of God in his eyes.

3. A young father gazing fondly on his wife and child.

4. A young mother sending her child off lovingly to school.

5. An old man (I myself am old) gazing into the distance, remembering happy experiences.

6. An employer showing kindness to someone working for him.

7. A shopkeeper greeting a customer with a happy smile.

8. A person (man or woman) in prayer, expressing love and bliss.

9. Two people at a tea table, showing joy after giving something to eat to a poor man.

10. A person rescuing a trapped animal, with love in his or her eyes.

These are ideas, only, but they may inspire many more. Are you interested?

Con amore e ammirazione,
swami kriyananda

Soon after, Swami and Raffaele met in person. I wonder if anyone had ever expressed before so much gratitude for his paintings or so much eagerness to meet him.

Swamiji commissioned Raffaele to do a few paintings for Ananda. One is the portrait of Jesus and Krishna together that is now used on the altar of the Ananda centers in India. Another was a painting of Our Lady of Guadalupe, that Swamiji used as the cover for his book, *A Pilgrimage to Guadalupe.*

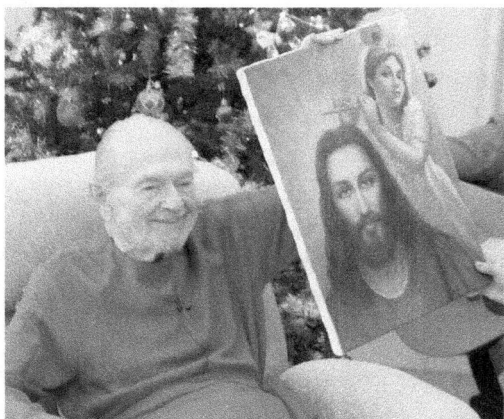

Raffaele told Swamiji, "Your words have banished years of doubt about my artistic skills. To have someone like you appreciating my art this way gives me the strength to keep going and not give up."

In India, Swami was scheduled to give a public talk at the National Centre for the Performing Arts in Mumbai. We arrived a few days early so that Swamiji could be well rested for the event. This also gave the local devotees the opportunity to meet and spend time with him.

We were having tea in the lobby of the hotel. For the entertainment of the guests, a young woman was playing soft music on a grand piano. We didn't notice her until Swami pointed her out. She played very nicely and after tea, he thanked her for the music. He told her he had composed over four-hundred pieces of music. When she showed keen interest, he asked us to bring him the sheet music for one of his favorites, *Love Is a Magician*.

As she started to read through the music, Swami asked if she wanted to play it. He stood close behind her while she played, singing quietly. He pointed to the music or showed her with his voice subtle points she might not have noticed. By the time they finished, her energy was much more relaxed and happy than before.

The next day, the pianist greeted Swamiji in the lobby and thanked him for the opportunity to play his music.

"I'm speaking tomorrow at the National Centre for the Performing Arts. Would you like to perform that song with me?"

She couldn't believe the offer! She thanked Swamiji, but said she wasn't sure she would be able to. She also felt unsure about performing on such short notice. One could see that the initial excitement at the invitation began to give way to nervousness and doubt.

"This could be a good opportunity for you, if you can." He continued, trying to boost her confidence, "And don't worry, I know you'll do a good job."

As it happened, she was able to arrange it and the next evening accompanied Swami while he sang.

She had to go back to work before the program ended, and we left the next day. We didn't see her again, so I can't share her perspective on meeting Swami. Maybe he helped her fulfill a dream to perform for a large audience in a prestigious hall. Perhaps Swamiji wanted her to experience a kind of music she might not have played before. In any case, I believe he planted a seed in her of her own potential to use music to uplift people's consciousness.

Swami encouraged creativity of all kinds, no matter how small or trivial it might seem. In my case, I began making Kriya *malas* for meditation, mostly just for fun, but also to bring in a little extra income. When I showed Swamiji my first finished mala, he expressed delight that I was being creative in this way.

He wanted to take me shopping at a bead store. At first I refused. I didn't want to put him to the trouble, but he insisted. It turned out to be great fun for the both of us. We were like kids in a candy store. *Let's buy this! Let's also get that!* I couldn't tell who was more excited, Swami or I. After that, I often sat next to Swami making malas, when he was reading or resting.

Whenever I had a few ready, he would gather them in his hand, lift them to his spiritual eye and bless them. Giving them back to me, he would make comments like, "Well done, keep going."

When we were in Los Angeles and Swami was working on a script for a movie of Yogananda's life, we met with a few potential directors. Some were well-known; others not. For Swamiji, fame, or the lack of it, was not the deciding factor.

It came out that one director Swami was keen on had, some years earlier, made an "off-color" film. Because of that, most of those involved in the project said we shouldn't hire him. Swami listened respectfully to their point of view, then said simply, "For this very reason it could be spiritually beneficial for him to work on this movie."

Later, Swami said to me, "I don't care what he has done in the past. Only what will help him in the future. He is a good man."

For several reasons the project never took off and the movie is yet to be made.

Speaking of movies, it might interest you to know that Swami's three favorites are all by Walt Disney. He had others that he liked, but these are the ones we watched, and re-watched, most often: *Bambi*, *Cinderella*, and *Lady and the Tramp*.

Once I was in a hurry to get ready to go out for lunch with Swamiji. As a brahmacharini, I consciously chose not to pay much attention to the way I looked. That morning I dressed myself in a way I deemed "good enough." When Swamiji saw me he exclaimed, "At least comb your hair!"

I knew Swami was not suggesting I become vain or preoccupied about my looks. He was correcting my inner attitude, not my outer appearance. He wanted me to understand that renunciation need not exclude an appreciation for beauty.

Just as God created this universe in perfect harmony and balance, Swamiji felt it was our responsibility also to manifest these same qualities in everything we do. Our inner attitudes and the way we carry ourselves generate a subtle magnetism that attracts from the universe a similar response. Be it the clothes we wear, the houses we live in, the way we walk, or the attitudes we express, to Swamiji, it was all art. As he would say, "Everyone is an artist."

Swamiji would often go up to perfect strangers and thank them for wearing a beautiful color of tie, shirt, dress, or saree. The way we present ourselves to the world, Swami suggested, should be seen as a service to others.

He felt that the way people as a whole dressed influenced the overall direction of society. He didn't favor

many of the current fashions. He felt men, for example, were fast losing the concept of being *gentlemanly.* Looking around a restaurant once, he commented, "I'm surprised men don't wear jackets anymore. It brings out their refinement when they dress up in that way."

Swami had three homes: in Italy, India, and the United States. Each had its own unique energy. The one purpose behind the furniture and decorations he chose was to create an uplifted environment for himself and all those who came there.

Color was especially important to him because of the way it affects energy and consciousness. Bright, vivid, vibrant colors were his favorites. One reason he changed the color for the Nayaswami Order from ochre to blue he describes in his book:

> Blue suggests calmness, kindness, and an expansive consciousness. Blue should, however, convey warm feeling and should not be, for example, a steely blue. A bright (not dark) royal blue seems to me the perfect shade for expressing the renunciate attitude I have in mind.

About a painting he had recently bought, Swami said, "I look at paintings not as objects, but as friends. Just as you would invite a good friend to spend time with you, in the same way you should invite the right painting into your home."

Not only paintings, but many objects in his house were, to Swami, friends. When shopping, he would feel the energy and consciousness that went into making something. Only if it resonated with him would he "invite" that object into his home.

Shopping with Swamiji was always both an adventure and a lesson in attunement to vibration and beauty. He entered a shop only if he felt magnetically drawn to it. Once inside, he would see what items called out to him and head straight for that vortex of energy. If it wasn't something he needed himself, he might buy it to give to someone else.

In fact, there was rarely a shopping trip when he didn't buy gifts for others!

God Helping God

Over the years that I served Swami, I witnessed the countless ways in which he was a divine channel of help to anyone who had the good karma to come into contact with him, whether a total stranger or someone who had been close to him for years.

"It is when I am helping others that I feel the greatest bliss," Swamiji would say.

Here are a few stories that are still vivid in my mind.

A wealthy couple and their two children had recently moved into the community. They came to see Swami about a business project they had in mind. They described their vision and the details, which had all been worked out. The business they envisioned had a huge potential to benefit Ananda, both financially and in making it known. The couple had the resources and experience to make it happen.

Business has never been a particular interest of mine, but even I got caught up in their enthusiasm!

Swamiji listened carefully to everything they had to say. When they finished, he sat still and silent for a moment. I felt he was inwardly watching the whole thing play out in their lives. Finally he said, "What you have proposed is a very good idea. But I don't think it will benefit either of you spiritually."

A deep silence permeated the room. Then he continued. "You have come to a point in your lives where your good karma has led you to become disciples of Master. You have been initiated into Kriya Yoga. You have moved into a spiritual community and are now surrounded by people who want only what is best for you. Why sacrifice all that for a project that will undo everything you have worked all these incarnations to achieve?"

It was obvious the couple were deeply disappointed. They had expected his full support. It had never even occurred to them that Swami would refuse to give his blessings.

The meeting didn't last long after that, and all Swami's further suggestions fell on deaf ears. His advice was more than they could handle. Soon after, they moved out of the community and eventually left the path altogether.

Later, Swami said, "I knew I was taking a risk in speaking to them so frankly. But their spiritual life was at stake. They are my friends; I had to be sincere."

On another occasion he told me, "It amazes me how each person lives in his own reality. Few want advice. And even when they ask, only some are open to receive it."

He also said, "Try to listen for God's message with an open heart. Don't let your personal desires interfere with that process."

This helped me understand why, from the beginning, I was so careful not to close myself off from his direct, or indirect, guidance. My way was to tune in, not so much to the words he said to me, but to the vibration and the tone of his voice. To me, they carried the meaning more than the words themselves.

A woman who was new to the community asked for a private meeting with Swamiji. Very emotionally she began to tell him how unfairly she had been treated. She was very judgmental and critical in her perceptions of others. Before she got too far, Swami interrupted her.

"I won't let you speak like this! You are much too opinionated!" Forcefully he added, "Your emotions are so agitated, you should think twice before speaking so harshly of others!"

The woman was stunned by the intensity of Swami's rebuke, but had the courage to see that he was telling her the truth. "You are right, Swamiji. I'm sorry."

Now that he had her attention, his manner changed completely. So sweetly he said, "One is happier loving, happier in forgiving than in being bitter. I don't even know what it means to hate. We all have our shortcomings. Try not to judge others for theirs."

She burst into tears. Swamiji blessed her, saying, "You are always in my prayers. Just keep trying."

After she left, I said to Swami, "How wonderful that she was so open to what you had to say."

"I was very pleased to see that," Swami said. "In fact, she was right about how others have behaved toward her. But that wasn't the issue. It was her tendency to be so opinionated that needed correcting. She understood."

Then, jokingly, he added, "The big difference between avatars and the rest of humanity is that avatars have perceptions. Human beings have opinions."

After one of our long flights to India, Swami's body was unusually sore. Thinking a massage would help, we arranged for Pawan, a young masseur, to come to the house. We didn't have a massage table, and Pawan didn't bring one, so I covered Swami's bed with towels to keep the oil from staining the sheets.

I came back an hour later when Pawan was just finishing. "That was very good," Swami said. "Can you come back next week?" Pawan smiled and nodded his head that typical Indian way.

"Next time, though, could you bring a massage table? It would be more comfortable than the bed."

"Sir, I don't have a table," Pawan said. "I can't afford to buy one. I work at a spa and give extra massages in my spare time. My wife is pregnant and with the baby coming we need the extra money."

"In that case," Swami said, "I'd like to buy you a massage table. How much does one cost?"

Pawan was stunned, but managed to respond, "A few thousands rupees, I think. But I'm not sure, Sir."

"Find out and let me know. I'll pay for it."

It wasn't unusual for Swami to be this generous, but I sensed something more was going on here. After Pawan left, I told Swami, "Your generosity is such an inspiration to me!"

He answered, "Generosity is one person giving to another. That's not how I see it. Everyone is a part of me, an extension of myself."

The following week, when Pawan returned, the first thing Swami asked was, "Have you found out how much a massage table costs?"

Shyly Pawan said, "Yes, sir, but it is much more expensive than I thought." He named a figure that to him was a fortune.

"Well, that is more than I expected," Swami said. "But I said I would buy it for you, and I will." He opened his wallet, counted out the rupees, and handed them to Pawan. "I hope this will help you to support your family better."

Pawan accepted the money with a look of total disbelief on his face. No doubt he'd thought that when Swami heard the actual price, he would change his mind. I helped Swami lie down on the bed for the massage, then came back an hour later.

Pawan was in the bathroom washing his hands. I whispered to Swami, "I don't think Pawan will want you to pay for this massage. You have already given him so much."

"Of course I'll pay for it," Swami said. "He has done a good job and must be compensated."

As I expected, Pawan didn't want to be paid, but Swami kept insisting that he had no choice but to accept. He bowed his head and pronamed to Swami.

I accompanied Pawan to the door. He seemed unusually thoughtful. "Are you okay?" I asked him.

Hesitantly, he replied, "I was raised in an orphanage. I don't even know who my parents are. Growing up I had one burning desire: to feel the love of a father. Until today I had never experienced it. What Swamiji did for me, nobody has ever done before. He has fulfilled something very deep in my heart."

My eyes filled with tears as I said goodbye to him. "My best wishes to your wife, the baby, and for you as a new father."

I rushed back upstairs to Swami's room to tell him what Pawan had told me. Swamiji, too, was moved to tears. Quietly he said, "I'm so happy for him."

I have often wondered, in episodes like this one with Pawan, was Swami simply being used by God? Or was he consciously aware of all the reasons behind what he did or said? Only one time did I ask him.

Swami gave advice to a man he had just met which turned out to be *exactly* what that man needed to hear. "How did you know?" I asked Swami.

"I didn't. I just felt from within to say it," Swamiji said simply.

We were spending a few days at the Le Méridien Hotel in Pune. For Swami's afternoon walk, he decided to visit some of the shops inside the hotel. We entered a Kashmiri shop, the kind that has a great variety of items.

Swami had been encouraging me to start wearing a yellow sapphire. I was never comfortable with him spending money on me and I was afraid he intended to buy one for me. Sure enough, he went straight to the shopkeeper and asked for a yellow sapphire.

The moment Swamiji showed interest in buying something that expensive, the shopkeeper seemed to pounce on him like a hungry hyena! He started pushing one thing after another onto Swamiji in a way I thought most unpleasant. It was more than I could handle. My protective instinct took over and I tried to get Swamiji out of the shop, but with no success.

When Swamiji mentioned that he was a disciple of Paramhansa Yogananda, the shopkeeper tried to use the "spiritual angle" to get him to buy more.

I was shooting menacing glances at the shopkeeper, but Swamiji just smiled and pointed to the next thing that interested him. I was boiling over with frustration at the way the shopkeeper took advantage of Swami's enthusiasm, while Swamiji, oblivious to the man's greed, showered him with thanks and praise for being so helpful.

This was not the shining hour of my spiritual life! Nonetheless, I felt I had to protect Swami's interests. He said, "Narayani, I think this yellow sapphire will help you. I want to buy it for you." I protested strongly, telling Swami how much I disliked that *particular* yellow sapphire. But his mind was already made up.

Finally, it occurred to me: Swami is doing more here than just shopping! I said to myself, "*Relax!*" and walked around the shop, trying to cool myself down. When I returned to Swami, there on the counter was the yellow sapphire, a red pashmina shawl, and an aquamarine bracelet.

Beaming at me, Swamiji said, "These are going to be gifts for someone."

When he took out his credit card, the shopkeeper said, "Could you pay with cash instead?" The barely suppressed volcano within me began to rumble again! As calm as ever, Swamiji said, "Sure." Then added, "But I don't think I have enough cash. Perhaps we could do the rest by card?"

When Swamiji took out his shiny Swarovski pen to sign the credit receipt, the shopkeeper exclaimed, "What a beautiful pen!"

Without the slightest hesitation Swami said, "Here, take it." The shopkeeper grabbed it and quickly put it in his pocket. Needless to say, this didn't sit well with me. But by now the absurdity of the situation made me aware that Swami was at work here. I don't know if there was a lesson for the shopkeeper, but for sure there was one for me.

When I meditated on the incident later that evening I thought of things I'd missed at the time. I suspect that shopkeeper has had to fight for every little penny he has ever earned, perhaps at times using dishonest means.

Instead of resenting that man's greedy energy, as I did, Swami showered him with love and praise, and cooperated with his every request. Perhaps no one had ever given to that man in the way Swami did — without fighting, haggling, or deceit.

Obviously, I had a lesson to learn: You cannot overcome the negative energy of others by injecting more negativity of your own. When others are being negative, that, more than ever, is the time they need our compassion and love.

A month later, a small group of us were celebrating my birthday over dinner. When dessert was served, Swami excused himself and went into his room. Emerging a moment later with a big grin on his face and a bag in his hand, he said, "Happy birthday, Narayani! I hope you like your gifts."

Perhaps you've already guessed what was inside: a red pashmina shawl and an aquamarine bracelet!

Once in Rome we were staying at a hotel on the piazza of the Pantheon. It was perfect for Swamiji because he could just step out the door and join the crowd in the piazza for his daily walks. He enjoyed seeing how uniquely God expresses Himself in each human being.

On our first walk, we saw a young woman begging just outside the hotel. She had no hands and no feet. It was heart-wrenching to see her sitting there, especially to see the profound sadness in her eyes.

"I hope she has some friends or family to help her," I said to Swami.

"I feel sorry for her, too," Swami said. "I wonder, though, what divine laws she must have broken in her previous lives to be born this way?"

In no way was Swami suggesting that we should be uncompassionate or indifferent to her suffering. Only that we not get emotionally entangled, because all is *right*, and *fair*, in God's love.

The next day, we saw her again, sitting in the same place as before. As we walked by, I sent her silent prayers of love and friendship.

On our last day, she wasn't there. "I wonder what happened to her?" Swami said. "I had something to tell her."

He went to the hotel doorman. "Have you see the woman who sits there and begs?" Swami asked, pointing to the spot. "Do you know whom I mean?"

The doorman said he had never seen her. Nonetheless, Swami said, "Could you please do me a favor? The next time you see her, give her this." He handed the doorman a one-hundred Euro bill. "And please tell her that she needn't be afraid. God loves her very much." Those last words brought tears to Swami's eyes.

One can only imagine what that poor woman goes through every day. Nothing we could give her could fully alleviate her suffering. But perhaps Swami's message would touch her soul and that would be the start of a change in her karma.

Swamiji usually needed a wheelchair to move through the airport. I'd follow behind him with both our carry-ons. Passing through airports was always a hectic affair for me. I had to deal with both our security checks, which meant opening and closing our bags, and removing all the electronics, all the while keeping an eye on Swamiji to make sure he was all right. Sometimes we traveled with others who helped, but towards the end it was often just the two of us.

After jumping through all these hoops, arriving at the gate an hour before boarding was something I looked forward to.

Once, on a trip from India to Europe, we had a short layover in Dubai. After the usual hassles, we reached the gate. I was eager for a few quiet hours. Just as I settled into my seat, Swami nudged me with his elbow and said quietly, "Look at that woman over there. Is she crying? Could you go over and ask her if she is all right?"

I went and sat down next to the lady. "Do you need any help?" I asked. Between sobs she told me that this was the first time she had traveled alone. Now she had lost her passport and didn't know what was going to happen. She couldn't go anywhere without it and was worried and afraid.

I comforted her the best I could. When I thought my job was done, I came back to Swami. I explained her situation and assured him that she'd be fine. The police were coming to help her and it would all be straightened out.

Feeling pretty good about my "act of kindness," I was ready to get back to my peace and quiet. But before I could settle in, Swamiji said, "Why don't you sit with her until she calms down? She could really use a friend."

So I went and sat with her, trying to distract her from giving in to her fears. But I was too distracted with my own worries: I can't believe I've left Swami all alone. He is my first responsibility. I should be there with him. What if he needs to go to the bathroom, or gets thirsty, or . . . ??!

As soon as the lady began to calm down, and even to smile a little, I assured her that we were "just over there" for any help she might need. I went back to Swamiji feeling extremely satisfied with the positive results of my fifteen minutes with her.

Once again I assured him that all was well, and there was nothing to worry about. But for him, that was not enough. Once more he said, "Please do not leave her alone until we are called to board. She still needs us."

This being his third request, it dawned on me that Swamiji was not only helping *that* lady. This was also for me. When, once again, I sat down next to her, I suddenly felt an expanding joy in my heart. The more *consciously* I tried to comfort her, the more that joy grew. The more *consciously* I gave love to her, the deeper that joy became. The thought spontaneously arose, "This is the joy that comes from helping others."

When they finally announced our flight, it was hard to pull myself away from her.

As I gathered our things and helped Swami to the gate, he said simply, "I'm so glad you stayed with her. Our inner happiness increases when we try also to make other people happy."

Swami felt that woman's suffering and wanted to help her. But instead of having me take him over to her, he sent me. I have come to realize that whenever Swami asked me to do something, it wasn't just because he wanted it done, or because he couldn't do it himself — it was because it would benefit me spiritually.

It is one thing to be *told* about joy, even by Swami, and quite another to *experience* joy for oneself. In giving me the chance to help that woman, he gave me a taste of how he feels *all* the time.

For Swamiji, helping others didn't require any special thought or effort. It was simply who he was, as natural to him as breathing.

There was no need for me to explain to Swami what I had just experienced.

All I said was, "Thank you, Swamiji."

Blessing Elisabeth Rohm in Finding Happiness

Shurjo, Pune, 2012

You Will Need Help

hen I took my brahmacharya vows, I felt I could live that way forever. A life offered *fully* to God, without reservations or distractions. Or so I thought.

There are certain souls we meet who change the course of our lives. Shurjo, was, for me, one such soul. We met in 2009 after Swamiji moved to his house in Pune. He, too, had taken the vow of brahmacharya and was living in the monastery there. I recognized him immediately as an old friend.

Our vows didn't allow for social contact, so we interacted only when our areas of seva coincided, which wasn't often. He supervised construction, and was responsible for upkeep and maintenance of the property. My focus, of course, was Swamiji.

Even though traveling with Swamiji took me away from Pune for many months of the year, each time

I returned, I felt a deeper friendship with Shurjo and an increasing call to give outward expression to what I felt within.

This created *tremendous* conflict within me. My service to Swami was based on complete attunement with him. Would sharing my life with Shurjo change my vibration to such an extent that I could no longer serve Swami in the same way?

This was one of the hardest periods of my life. My days I spent with Swamiji; my nights I spent in prayer. If this call to be with Shurjo was only a *passing* karma, or a temptation to be resisted, I preferred to fight it out alone. So I said nothing to Swami about my inner struggle.

Finally, after six months, it was clear to me that my connection to Shurjo was a karma that had to be faced and decided. It was then I brought the issue to Swamiji.

He listened to my words, but more than that, I felt he was listening for Master's voice behind my own. When I finished, he said only, "Let me meditate on it." We said good night. He went to his meditation room. I went to bed, but didn't sleep a wink.

At 5:00 a.m. the next morning, Swamiji came to my room. "I think it would be good for you to be with

Shurjo," he said. "If you are going to serve Master in the way I see for you, you will need help. Shurjo can help you."

The rest of the morning passed as if nothing new had occurred. At lunchtime, Swami asked, "So, when are you getting married?"

I was shocked! "Married?! No, Swami, not yet! We barely know each other. We have to try it and see how it works out. In a few years, if it seems right, perhaps then we can get married." I babbled on for a while about how the transition would happen, how Shurjo and I would gradually get acquainted, how he would fit into my life with Swamiji. I had it all planned out!

Swamiji interrupted. "You can't wait a few years. You have to marry him now. As soon as we return to India."

We arrived in India three weeks later. By the end of our first week there, in October 2012, Shurjo and I were married. Only later did I understand why Swamiji was in such a hurry.

"After I am gone," he had told me, "you will need protection. Shurjo can protect you."

He moved into Swami's house in Gurgaon, where I was already living. Swami welcomed Shurjo completely, included him whenever he felt to, but both were comfortable with the fact that often it needed to be just Swami and me. There was no transition. Shurjo blended seamlessly into life with Swami.

Our wedding, Gurgaon, 2012

God's Call Within

S wami had made it clear that he was ready to leave whenever Master called him, but I thought he had more time before that call would come.

Those last months of his life were some of the most powerful, and intense, of my time with Swamiji. It was almost constant outward energy, without, it seemed, a moment to rest. It was tumultuous, not in a negative way, but a great deal happened in a short time.

Traveling, movies being made, many large public events, books being written, and, on top of all that, the many health challenges Swami faced. In the past, there had always been a few other people around, usually the leaders of whichever community we were in, who were close to Swami and shared responsibility for his personal well-being. But certain changes in India left a gap in

his care. His cook, secretary, and nurse each had their specific duties, but everything else was up to me.

It turned out to be Master's plan. Solitude was just what Swami needed at that time.

The intuitive flow between us was so well established, I knew what calls to return, which invitations to accept, where he would speak, the subjects for his talks, when to take a walk, whether to invite someone for tea.

Much of the time now he preferred not to have any people around him except me, and sometimes Shurjo.

I was so grateful for Shurjo. I made all the plans for Swami, but Shurjo had the executive skill to make it happen. I was in a foreign country and didn't know the native languages. Shurjo spoke several and knew how things worked. He took care of everything: tickets, cars, drivers, hotel check-in and check-out, keeping track of the money. He had the practical side covered so I could relax and focus just on Swami.

We stayed in Gurgaon only a few weeks, then moved to Swami's house in Pune. But those last months in India were a time of almost ceaseless travel, so we weren't at home very often.

We lived in a small cottage just a few steps from the back door of Swami's house. I put a baby monitor in his bedroom and turned it up loud enough to hear him breathe. I never left Swamiji at night until he was safe in bed. From the cottage I knew when he turned over or got up and walked around. If I thought something was wrong, or if he called my name, I could be with him in seconds.

Many nights he had trouble sleeping. I would go and make him some hot milk, give him a massage, or just sit next to him while he read until he felt tired enough to go to bed again. One night his blood sugar crashed and he nearly went into a coma. Most of all, though, he was just tired. *Very* tired. His body no longer responded to his willpower.

Inside the house, he could still walk from room to room, but I would always follow him, because he could fall at any moment. When we left the house, he usually had someone on each arm now. He could hardly support his own weight. He still did the energization exercises, but for many of them I would hold his waist to keep him upright and balanced.

Swamiji was still busy outwardly, but it was different. Before, he would get energy back from what he was

doing. Sometimes after a lecture, he would be so uplifted and speak of the joy of doing a great work for Master.
Now, the willingness was there, but the enthusiasm
was fading.

He seemed to be saying to Shurjo and me, "I've done
all I can. It is up to all of you now, to carry on."

He was in silence much of the time. I felt he was
listening inwardly to understand what these changes
meant in terms of his life, his discipleship, and his service to Master.

In precarious health, and in this mood, but still
willing to do whatever Master asked of him, Swami
traveled all over India. He had huge public events in
major cities: Delhi, Gurgaon, Chennai, Pune, Mumbai,
Bangalore, Kolkata. He had the magnetism to draw
thousands of people, most of them deeply sincere. Plus
there were informal gatherings with the local devotees.
It was his final effort to make his guru known in the
land of his birth.

More young people were coming, both from India
and from around the world. They followed Swamiji

from city to city. I think it was easier, with Shurjo and me there, for them to feel that Swamiji belonged to their generation, too.

Indians have great devotion for holy people and great faith in the power of their touch. In Bangalore, the moment the talk finished, the crowd surged around Swami, hoping to touch his feet. We were so blocked in that we could barely make it up the aisle to the front door of the hall. Shurjo saw there was no hope of getting to our car, so he grabbed the first available one, and asked the woman inside if she could take us back to our hotel. She had been at the lecture, but had never met Swami before and couldn't believe he was now sitting in her car!

One great hardship for Swami in those last years was the increasing loss of his hearing. He was almost entirely deaf in one ear. Then, on the plane flight from Kolkata to Mumbai, his "good ear" stopped working. When I spoke to him in a normal voice, even with his hearing aid, he could only see my lips moving. It seemed his senses were shutting down.

We went to a doctor who told us that sometimes this happens in older people. Maybe it would come back. Maybe it wouldn't.

During that time they were filming *The Answer*, a movie based on Swami's autobiography, *The New Path*. At that time, the script included Swamiji reminiscing about his life with Master. We were on our way to Mumbai to do some filming when his hearing went out. Eventually Swami was able to do the scene, but we had to write the questions on a board so he could read them, since he could hardly hear. The story line changed later, and that film wasn't used, but it came out pretty well.

Eventually, some hearing came back, but not as much as before.

No matter what the title of his lecture, all Swami wanted to talk about was Master. Many times the thought of his guru moved him so deeply, he had to stop speaking until his tears stopped flowing.

He ended all his lectures with the song, "Thy Light Within Us Shining." He would sit while he lectured, but stand for that song. He needed someone on each arm and often I supported him from the waist, too. Even though it was so difficult, I felt Swami had too much respect for the Divine Light to remain seated.

I often thought, *"He is the Light that is shining."*

Between each city, we would return to his home in Pune so he could rest and recover from the last event, and prepare himself for the one to come. Amazingly, he also spent time there reviewing, and sometimes revising, books and music he had written years before. He did new work, also—movie scripts, a novel, a complete study course.

For most of the years he had lived in India, he'd spent several weeks each January on vacation in Goa. He had a favorite hotel, the *Taj Exotica*. He loved the layout: small cottages, close together, but arranged in such a way that each had privacy. Usually up to a dozen people went with him, mostly Ananda leaders from around the world. He wanted the leaders to ask the hotel for the plans so we could build our communities in a similar way.

This time, though, when I asked whom he wanted to invite to Goa, he said, "No one." Just Shurjo and me. He didn't even want his nurse to come. "I'll be fine," he said. But I couldn't imagine not having her there, nor did she feel it was wise to let him go without her. So she came and stayed in the hotel next door. Every morning she checked his sugar levels, but otherwise we didn't see her.

We walked twice a day and had meals together, but Swamiji spent a lot of time alone, in silence. And when we were together, I kept the conversation light.

One day over lunch he read us a P.G. Wodehouse story! He was able to disconnect completely from his own work, the lectures he was doing, and whatever was happening at Ananda.

Goa, 2013

During these last months, Swami became increasingly direct in his advice and suggestions. Everything had to be accelerated because he knew he didn't have much time.

One evening we were sitting in silence watching the sun go down. "Narayani, promise me something," he said. "Never let anyone kill your spirit."

I didn't know why he made this sudden and unexpected request, but after a pause, I said, "I'll try, Swamiji."

With great seriousness he responded, "Good."

I knew he had expectations for my future that I would never have had for myself, but I didn't ask him to explain why he wanted me to promise. I rarely asked him for the "why" behind his comments, even if I didn't understand. It was up to him to decide what he wanted to share or withhold from me.

"Most people come with the hope of receiving from me," Swamiji told me. "It is appropriate for them to feel that way and it is my joy to give. You are unusual, though, for your only thought is to give to me. I can see now you have been coming with me, lifetime after lifetime, playing many different roles. But always by my side, helping me. That is why I am so comfortable having you around."

One day near the end of our stay in India, I received a phone call from one of the ashram residents. Swami Dattavadhut had just arrived and wanted to see Swamiji. He was taking his afternoon nap and usually I wouldn't disturb him, but this time it felt appropriate. Gently waking him, I told him about Dattavadhutji's arrival. They had met once before in Gurgaon and Swami got up at once, saying, "I'd love to see him. Please ask him to come immediately and we can have tea outside." Shurjo went to greet the swami and his two disciples and show them the way to the house.

Swami Dattavadhut spoke in Hindi and Shurjo translated, but the real conversation between the swamis was through their eyes. They were delighted to see each other again. They would look at each other, smile, and giggle. One could feel their mutual love and respect because of their shared love for God. It was both sweet and powerful to see them together.

"When I visited India in the '50s and '60s," Swamiji said to Dattavadhutji, "I used to see many more saints. Now I don't see them. Have they all gone to the Himalayas? Have you met any saints lately?"

"Yes!" Dattavadhutji said, emphatically. "You."

Later his disciple told us that Swami Dattavadhut spends almost all his time alone in the jungle, meditating and doing tapasya. He rarely comes out, and when he does, he has a specific purpose. One purpose this time was to see Swami Kriyananda. Their meeting lasted only half an hour. Much that happened between them, I think, was not visible to our eyes.

A few days later, Swamiji was rushed to the hospital with a kidney problem. That same day, Shurjo got a call from Dattavadhutji's disciple. He very much wanted to see Swamiji again. Unfortunately, that wasn't possible. Swami was sick in the hospital and scheduled to leave India soon. The visit would have to wait till Swami returned.

Many months later, Shurjo and I spoke with Swami Dattavadhut's disciple, Vanita. She told us that when Dattavadhutji was leaving Swamiji's house, he said to her, "Swami Kriyananda won't be in the body much longer. That is why I so urgently wanted to see him now."

Vanita also told us that on the very day, at almost the same moment Swamiji passed away, Dattavadhutji had called one of his disciples and asked him to find out if Swami Kriyananda was still living.

Swamiji had given Swami Dattavadhut the Hindi edition of *The Essence of the Bhagavad Gita*. After reading it, he said to Vanita, "To be able to explain so beautifully and insightfully the deep truths of the Gita, I think Swami Kriyananda must have been Ved Vyasa himself."

He also told her, "Several years ago I read the book, *The Imitation of Christ*. After meeting Swami Kriyananda I feel he might have been Thomas à Kempis in a former life."

It takes a saint to recognize a saint. The rest of us see only as much as they allow us to see. As Master says in one of his songs, "He knows, whom You let know."

With Vanita and Swami Dattavadhutji, 2013

Easter, Assisi, 2013

Moksha

hen we left India for Assisi in March 2013, none of us had the slightest inkling how close we were to the end. Swami had had many close calls with death, but each time he was called back by his guru to serve him a little longer.

Now, however, Swami's energy was unusually different. It felt like he was withdrawing from the world, with a level of detachment uncharacteristic of him. There was around him an air of fulfillment, a sense of completion. It was as if there was no need for him to engage with the world, no compulsion to create anything new, no reason to direct his energy outward, no service left undone. It was the inner world now that held his attention.

In April, Swami spent most of his time in silence. In the past, he would invite people over nearly every day. Now he hardly saw anyone except Shurjo and me. His withdrawal was so complete, he scarcely ate. Physically he was weak and increasingly fragile. Referring to his body, he said, "I feel like I'm disappearing."

Though outwardly silent, he was, I sensed, inwardly conversing with Master, surrendering Himself to His will. I have never felt Swami closer to his guru than during that month.

A few days before Easter, Swami asked me to play a recording of his oratorio, *Christ Lives*. When the music began, he closed his eyes and withdrew into the Christ consciousness. Looking at his beatific smile, I knew he was in bliss. I closed my eyes and sat in meditation next to him, hoping to feel some of what he was feeling.

When the song "The Temptation of Christ" began, I heard Swamiji whisper, "This is my favorite song." When it finished, he asked me to play it again. Then again. And again. He listened to it at least five times, with tears rolling down his cheeks. "I feel just like Jesus. No matter how many times he was tempted by Satan, he always chose God."

A few days later, he wrote the following email, which he sent to Ananda devotees around the world.

Dear Ones:

I wish I could bless each and every one of you with a happy Easter. Easter is a time symbolizing the eventual resurrection of our little, individual selves into the one, Infinite Self. I suggest at this time particularly that you study and meditate on the photograph of Master titled The Last Smile. And consider this amazing fact: He knew that in just a few moments he would be leaving his physical body forever! There is no thought of self in his eyes, of personal regret, of sorrow. Clearly visible in his eyes and in his facial expression is his unconditional love for all mankind; his readiness to return "again and again," as he put it, as long as one stray brother sits weeping by the wayside. Such love, for ego-centered humanity, is not even conceivable. And this was the love Jesus, too, felt for all humanity. People weep for him and his suffering on the cross. His suffering was only for humanity, that blindly rejects God's love and substitutes for it vengefulness and hatred!

I have been going through a personal Armageddon. Nothing in this world attracts me anymore. Nothing at all holds any pleasant memories — none of those experiences, whether interpersonal or outward in any way, holds the slightest attraction for me. Must I really live another five years, as has been predicted for me? I confess the very idea appalls me. I have done so much in my life to please God. The very hallmark of my nature has been enthusiasm, even though I've been always aware that I could never really accomplish anything significant in this world. Suddenly, now, I feel bereft of that enthusiasm. Maybe it's because my heart feels very tired. I want only to merge in God. The only lingering thought is that I would like to bring all of you with me. No, I am far from tired of you! I want only your freedom in God. But no, your worldly attachments, identities, and desires, I have to confess mean simply nothing to me, as my own mean nothing to me.

No, this doesn't mean I love you less. I love you much *more*, for I love that part of you which is eternally real.

But whether I succeed or fail in my projects is to me meaningless. All the things I once considered pleasurable are to me, now, *dis*pleasing. I want nothing that this world has to offer. People tell me I am famous: that phrase, to me, also is meaningless. People often marvel at all I have been able to accomplish in this life: to me, it all seems only dust.

If we must resurrect our souls, let it be from the delusion that anything in this cosmic dream holds some worthwhile reality for us. We are children of God: That is our sole reality!

Love, swami

The Last Smile

When I first read this email, a deep sadness came over me at the thought of Swamiji losing his enthusiasm. But after going over it several times more, I tuned in to what lay behind those words. Swamiji was ready to leave this earth. It wasn't an affirmation. It was his consciousness. St. Paul declared at the end of his life, "I have fought the good fight. I have finished the race. I have kept the faith." Swamiji, too, had finished his race.

There was nothing to be sad about. He was ready to merge back into God. He was free.

I wrote him the following note, which turned out to be the last e-mail we exchanged.

Dearest Swami:

I re-read again and again your e-mail and actually is really, really inspiring. I didn't enjoy that much when I read it first, because I don't enjoy to see you losing enthusiasm. . . . But at the same time, is quite inspiring to see you so ready and detached from your own personality and above all, personal experiences. Just ready to merge back in God.

I wish you could carry me with you when you go. I will be very happy for you when you leave this body. I know Master has a place for you next to him on the other side.

Thank you for sending this message. Really beautiful. I am now in front of Master's Last Smile picture.

I hope you never lose the enthusiasm for having me around. You are stock with me! :-)

Good night!

Narayani

Swami's reply:

> *Dear Narayani:*
>
> The word is stuck, not stock. And I'm very happy to be stuck as your stock friend!
>
> *love you, always,*
> *swami*

One of the movie scripts Swami worked on in Los Angeles was the story of Ananda. The last week of his life Shivani, the executive producer, brought Swami the finished movie, *Finding Happiness*. He invited a small group of friends to watch it with him at his house.

Finding Happiness is a creative blend of fact and fiction. The fiction is a journalist from New York who comes to California to find out about Ananda Village. The fact is the community itself, the people, and their stories. The journalist was an actress, but everyone else, including Swami, played himself or herself.

People who have had near-death experiences often talk about a "life review." Your whole life passes before you and you see the successes and failures, and all the lessons still to be learned. Watching that movie with Swami was like watching his life review. It captured in ninety minutes the fruit of Swami's sixty years of discipleship.

When *Finding Happiness* ended, there were tears in every eye. No one could speak. Many of those present had walked with Swamiji every step of the way and knew all the sacrifices he had made to manifest Ananda.

Finally, wiping the tears from his eyes, Swamiji broke the silence. "I see my Guru's dream fulfilled. I have accomplished all that I came to do. Master is very pleased."

That night Swami's heart was overflowing with joy. Whatever lingering doubt he might have had about pleasing his guru, *Finding Happiness* took it away. He had emptied himself out completely in service to Master.

"I'm so eager now to go to the astral world," he told me. Then paused for a few seconds. "Better still, to achieve final liberation — *moksha*."

His words did not feel like a wish. They were a prophecy.

Every morning Swami and I would meditate together at 6:30 a.m. But on April 21, when I went to his room as usual, I found him asleep in bed. In the meditation room, I saw a candle burning. Perhaps, I thought, he had woken up earlier and meditated by himself. Something, though, about the whole scene felt strange. Nothing specific, just a feeling.

I decided to go back downstairs and wait another half hour and see if Swami woke up on his own. Miriam, after checking on him, came to my room. "Swami is still asleep. Is everything okay?"

Soon we heard his footsteps and hurried back upstairs to greet him. Swami was sitting at his desk in front of his computer. It was his practice to check his emails first thing in the morning to see if someone needed to hear from him.

"Good morning, Swamiji," I said. "How are you feeling?"

He didn't reply, only smiled. When he turned towards me, I was struck by the look in his eyes. So distant. So far, far away. He got up from his desk and walked the few steps to his place at the dining room table. Each step was so deliberate, it seemed as if someone had pushed the slow-motion button. Miriam, sensing that something wasn't right, asked if she could check his blood sugar.

"Anything," Swamiji said.

His levels were perfectly normal, so she started walking toward the kitchen. I sat down next to Swamiji. In the one second it took me to turn my head towards him, his whole body tensed up in a wave rising from below, some sort of seizure.

"Miriam! Come back!" I shouted. She was there in a few seconds. By then Swamiji's whole body had relaxed and he sat slumped in his chair.

"Perhaps he is okay now," I said to her. But Miriam couldn't find a pulse or a heartbeat and as we watched, the color began to fade from his face.

"Breathe, Swamiji, breathe!" Miriam literally shouted at him.

Jaidhara, who had been in the kitchen cooking breakfast for Swami, rushed downstairs to get Shurjo, then ran to the Temple to get Kirtani and Anand. Miriam had been continuously chanting AUM in Swamiji's right ear. She asked Shurjo to take over and soon we saw Swami lift his head.

He was coming back! As he began to breathe, we carried him on his chair to his bedroom, and laid him on the bed. By this time Kirtani and Anand had arrived. For fifteen minutes we all chanted AUM aloud, Shurjo directly into Swami's right ear.

Swami took one breath. Then for several seconds, nothing. Then another breath. Then again, nothing. We shifted him onto his side, hoping it would help him breathe. Again, nothing. So we returned him to his back.

He opened his eyes just a little bit. For a few moments, he looked straight at me. Then his eyes closed again. There was one last, long exhalation.

Anand said, "I think he is gone."

Only then, for the first time, did it occur to me that this was not just another crisis. I sat on the floor at the foot of his bed to meditate. Before I could sink into the emptiness Swami's passing left in my heart, that void was filled by a pure, perfect Love. It was not coming *from* Swami; it *was* Swami.

The knowing came, "How much Swamiji loves us all!"

Swamiji's passing, April 21, 2013

Door of My Heart

oon after, the grief and sorrow caught up with me. Two days later, a friend called to tell me that he had dreamed about Swamiji and had a message for me. In the dream, he, Swami, and I were in the Temple talking together. My cell phone rang. Caller ID showed the name "Swami Kriyananda."

I was about to answer it when Swamiji said to me, "What are you doing?"

"I'm trying to take your call."

"If you want to communicate with me, you'll need to use this phone." In his hand was a *pink* phone. Pink is the color for the heart. In other words, "If I want to communicate with Swami, I need to use my heart."

I felt this was a message not only for me, but for all of us.

My heart remembers that my first meeting with Swami, through his music, and my last moment with him after his passing were exactly the same: an experience of his *perfect* love.

A curious fact about Swamiji's passing was that even after his last exhalation, inwardly, I didn't feel it was his time to go. It wasn't that I couldn't accept his passing. He was gone and I had to live with that.

But I couldn't disregard the feeling either, because it was the kind of feeling I have experienced many times and learned to trust. I needed to understand what took place that day.

I have come to believe that Swami's death wasn't "scheduled" for that day. It was a *special grace*, a blessing from his guru. He would willingly have continued to serve for a few years longer, writing more books, perhaps making that movie on Master's life, and who knows what else?

His essential work, though, was finished. He had more than fulfilled his guru's commission to him, "You have a great work to do."

I remember how much Swamiji cherished Master's words to him:

"You have pleased me very much. I want you to know that."

Painting by Nayaswami Jyotish

The End

Paramhansa Yogananda

Paramhansa Yogananda, author of *Autobiography of a Yogi*, came to the West from India in 1920, bringing a revolutionary vision of how to live. He lectured across the United States drawing thousands, and filling the largest auditoriums in the country. During the three decades he lived in America, he met many of the well-known figures of the time: President Calvin Coolidge, industrialist Henry Ford, and agricultural inventor Luther Burbank. Yogananda initiated Mahatma Gandhi into Kriya Yoga, the most advanced of the meditation techniques he taught. He is widely known as the "Father of Yoga" in the West.

Even after Yogananda's passing in 1952, his *Autobiography of a Yogi* continues to inspire influential people such as George Harrison, Gene Roddenberry (creator of the Star Trek series), and Steve Jobs. This book, translated into 34 languages, has helped start and continues to sustain the current spiritual renaissance seen in the West.

Swami Kriyananda

Swami Kriyananda was a direct disciple of Paramhansa Yogananda, author of *Autobiography of a Yogi*. Kriyananda dedicated his life to sharing Yogananda's revolutionary teachings of Self-realization and helping people bring spirituality into their daily life.

At Yogananda's request, Kriyananda devoted his life to lecturing, editing, and writing. He wrote over 150 books, available in 100 countries and translated into 30 languages. In addition he composed some 450 pieces of music.

Inspired by Yogananda's vision of what he called "world brotherhood colonies," in 1968 Swami Kriyananda founded the first of what are now seven Ananda spiritual communities worldwide. His dedication to truth has inspired people the world over to seek a deeper experience of their highest Self and to awaken their true potential.

Ananda

Ananda is a global movement dedicated to the realization that *joy is within you*. The word *Ananda* means "ever-new joy." Ananda is based on the scientific yoga teachings brought by Paramhansa Yogananda, with practical applications in daily life including how to be happy, how to be a success, spiritualizing relationships, health and healing, and more.

Ananda was founded in 1968 by Swami Kriyananda. It began in the Sierra Nevada foothills of California in what became known as Ananda Village, a spiritual community soon to celebrate its 50th year. Ananda has now grown to include centers, meditation groups, and spiritual communities throughout the USA, Europe, Asia, and India.

Today Ananda is led by Spiritual Directors Nayaswami Jyotish Novak — whom Swami Kriyananda named as his spiritual successor — and his wife, Nayaswami Devi.

Further Explorations

CRYSTAL CLARITY PUBLISHERS

If you enjoyed this title, Crystal Clarity Publishers invites you to deepen your spiritual life through many additional resources based on the teachings of Paramhansa Yogananda. We offer books, e-books, audiobooks, yoga and meditation videos, and a wide variety of inspirational and relaxation music composed by Swami Kriyananda.

See a listing of books below, visit our secure website for a complete online catalog, or place an order for our products.

crystalclarity.com

800.424.1055 | clarity@crystalclarity.com

1123 Goodrich Blvd. | Commerce, CA 90022

ANANDA WORLDWIDE

Crystal Clarity Publishers is the publishing house of Ananda, a worldwide spiritual movement founded by Swami Kriyananda, a direct disciple of Paramhansa Yogananda. Ananda offers resources and support for your spiritual journey through meditation instruction, webinars, online virtual community, email, and chat.

Ananda has more than 150 centers and meditation groups in over 45 countries, offering group guided meditations, classes and teacher training in meditation and yoga, and many other resources.

In addition, Ananda has developed eight residential communities in the US, Europe, and India. Spiritual communities are places where people live together in a spirit of cooperation and friendship, dedicated to a common goal. Spirituality is practiced in all areas of daily life: at school, at work, or in the home. Many Ananda communities offer internships during which one can stay and experience spiritual community firsthand.

For more information about Ananda communities or meditation groups near you, please visit ananda.org or call 530.478.7560.

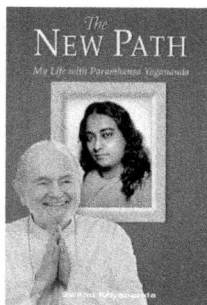

THE NEW PATH
My Life with Paramhansa Yogananda
Swami Kriyananda

Winner of the 2010 Eric Hoffer Award for Best Self-Help/Spiritual Book
Winner of the 2010 USA Book News Award for Best Spiritual Book

The New Path is a moving revelation of one man's search for lasting happiness. After rejecting the false promises offered by modern society, J. Donald Walters found himself (much to his surprise) at the feet of Paramhansa Yogananda, asking to become his disciple. How he got there, trained with the Master, and became Swami Kriyananda makes fascinating reading.

The rest of the book is the fullest account by far of what it was like to live with and be a disciple of that great man of God.

Anyone hungering to learn more about Yogananda will delight in the hundreds of stories of life with a great avatar and the profound lessons they offer. This book is an ideal complement to *Autobiography of a Yogi*.

FAITH IS MY ARMOR
The Life of Swami Kriyananda
by Nayaswami Devi Novak

This is the story of a man who has achieved extraordinary victories in his life—not with weapons, but with moral and spiritual courage. The life of Swami Kriyananda is the story of a man who has, to an amazing degree, demonstrated spiritual courage, determination in the face of great obstacles, and personal sacrifice for an ideal.

Faith Is My Armor tells the complete story of his life: from his childhood in Rumania, to his desperate search for meaning in life, and to his training under his great Guru, the Indian Master, Paramhansa Yogananda. As a youth of twenty-two, he first met and pledged his discipleship to Yogananda, entering the monastery Yogananda had founded in Southern California.

In the over sixty years since then, Swami Kriyananda traveled and lived around the world, lecturing in five languages, wrote over 100 books and 400 pieces of music, and founded seven spiritual communities in the United States, Europe, and India.

It also recounts the drama of the powerful opposition and attacks he faced as he strove to fulfill the mission his Guru had bestowed upon him.

This book will bring inspiration and hope to all who read it, and renewed faith in the power of God in our lives.

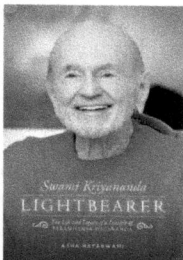

LIGHTBEARER: SWAMI KRIYANANDA
The Life and Legacy of a disciple of
Paramhansa Yogananda
by Asha Nayaswami

Swami's life was a triumphant life, but not an easy one. Plagued by ill-health, financial challenges, and years of bitter estrangement from fellow disciples, his life story is told in the struggle as well as the victory. A great soul incarnates to awaken faith in our own spiritual potential. Asha writes, "A great wave of Divine Light is sweeping over the planet. If you tune in to that Light, you, too, will become an instrument of that Light."

This first-hand account of life with Swami Kriyananda is more than a biography. It's a guidebook for spiritual living, a path of light that all may follow. And it's a labor of love by Asha that has been forty-four years in the making.

SWAMI KRIYANANDA
As We Have Known Him
by Asha Praver

In this "biography of consciousness," Swami Kriyananda's remarkable qualities are revealed with breathtaking clarity—love for God, divinely guided strength, joy in the face of adversity, humor, wisdom, compassion, and unconditional love.

Here, in some two hundred stories spanning more than forty years, personal reminiscences and private moments with this beloved teacher become universal life lessons for us all.

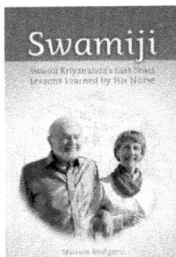

SWAMIJI
Swami Kriyananda's Last Years; Lessons
      Learned by His Nurse
by Miriam Rodgers

Paramhansa Yogananda once said to a group
of disciples: "You must not let the symphony
of your life go unfinished."

This phrase perfectly describes the last years
of Swami Kriyananda's life, which were a crescendo of divine
love and untiring service to humanity.

In this profoundly moving biographical account filled with
never before heard stories, you'll glimpse the interior castle of
Swami Kriyananda's consciousness. Rodgers shares an intimate
and up-close look at lessons she learned through her connection
as Swami Kriyananda's nurse for the last fourteen years of his life.

Throughout history, the saints alone are the true custodians of
religion. Saints like Swami Kriyananda draw their understanding from the direct experience of truth and of God, not from
superficial reasoning or book learning.

www.ingramcontent.com/pod-product-compliance
Lightning Source LLC
Chambersburg PA
CBHW070328090426
42733CB00012B/2407